DESIGN STUDIO
2021 VOLUME 1

Design Studio Vol. 1 Everything Needs to Change: Architecture and the Climate Emergency is printed on Fenner Paperbrite 260gsm and Revive Offset Recycled 120gsm paper, FSC® Recycled 100% post-consumer waste. Papers Carbon Balanced by the World Land Trust. Printed with eco-friendly high-quality vegetable-based inks by Pureprint Group, the world's first carbon neutral printer.

© RIBA Publishing, 2021

Published by RIBA Publishing, 66 Portland Place, London, W1B 1AD

ISBN 978 1 85946 965 1
ISSN 2634-4653

British Library Cataloguing-in-Publication Data
A catalogue record for this book is available from the British Library.

Commissioning Editor: Alex White
Assistant Editor: Clare Holloway
Production: Sarah-Louise Deazley
Designed and typeset by Linda Byrne
Printed and bound by Pureprint Group

www.ribapublishing.com

About the Editors **V**

Editor's Note
Sofie Pelsmakers and
Nick Newman **IX**

ARTICLES

Creating Change with Impact:
An Architect's Manifesto
Dorte Mandrup **1**

Not Opposites: A Conversation
with Hiroshi Sambuichi
on Architecture and Nature
Andrew Barrie **12**

Think Before You Build
Kari Kytölä, Paulina Sawczuk
and Satu Huuhka **25**

Movement Building: Activism
in an Age of Crisis
Tom Bennett **34**

The Sponge City: Planning,
Design and Political Design
Kongjian Yu **47**

Contesting the Architect's Role
through Radical Participatory
Design: A Discussion with
Al Borde and raumlabor
Mario Kolkwitz and Elina Luotonen
in conversation with David
Barragán and Markus Bader **57**

Transforming Education in a
Climate Emergency
Architects Climate Action Network
(ACAN) **66**

Architectural Learning for a
Sustainable Future
Elizabeth Donovan, Urszula
Kozminska, Nacho Ruiz Allen
and Thomas R. Hilberth **77**

Hope in the Burning World
Kasia Nawratek **87**

PROFILES

Towards a Zero Carbon Architecture
Mikhail Riches **99**

Radical Sustainable Architecture
Alex de Rijke at dRMM **105**

Co-housing Project
Siv Helene Stangeland **111**

Implementing Sustainability
Anders Lendager at Lendager Group **117**

CASE STUDIES

A Choreography of Bricks
Samira Rathod **124**

Adaptation Out of Necessity
Anyana Zimmerman and
Fabián Rodríguez Izquierdo **130**

Sustainability is Not Enough
Stephen Choi **138**

Final Word
Sofie Pelsmakers and
Nick Newman **144**

Contributors **148**

Recommended reading **150**

Index **151**

Image credits **154**

EVERY-THING NEEDS TO CHANGE

About the Editors

Sofie Pelsmakers is an environmental architect, educator and researcher, and the author of the *Environmental Design Pocketbook*. She is an expert in holistic sustainable architecture, actual performance of buildings over time (including validation methods), low energy, zero carbon buildings and retrofit, and sustainable design pedagogies. Sofie is actively engaged in making a difference in architecture by training the next generation of architects and influencing those in practice through her teaching, publications, and public speaking/workshops. She is currently Assistant Professor at Tampere University, Finland, where she chairs the Sustainable Housing Design research group.

Nick Newman is Director of Studio Bark and U-Build. His experience spans environmental architecture, climate activism, building performance evaluation and deep energy retrofits. He is a Passivhaus designer and has contributed to a number of journals and publications, including the *Environmental Design Pocketbook* and the *Passivhaus Designer's Manual*. He speaks regularly at events on behalf of the studio and was named a 'Rising Sustainability Star' by *Building* magazine in 2014. Nick is an advocate for radical responses to the Climate Emergency and was arrested in October 2019 for his involvement in the Extinction Rebellion protests, which brought central London to a standstill.

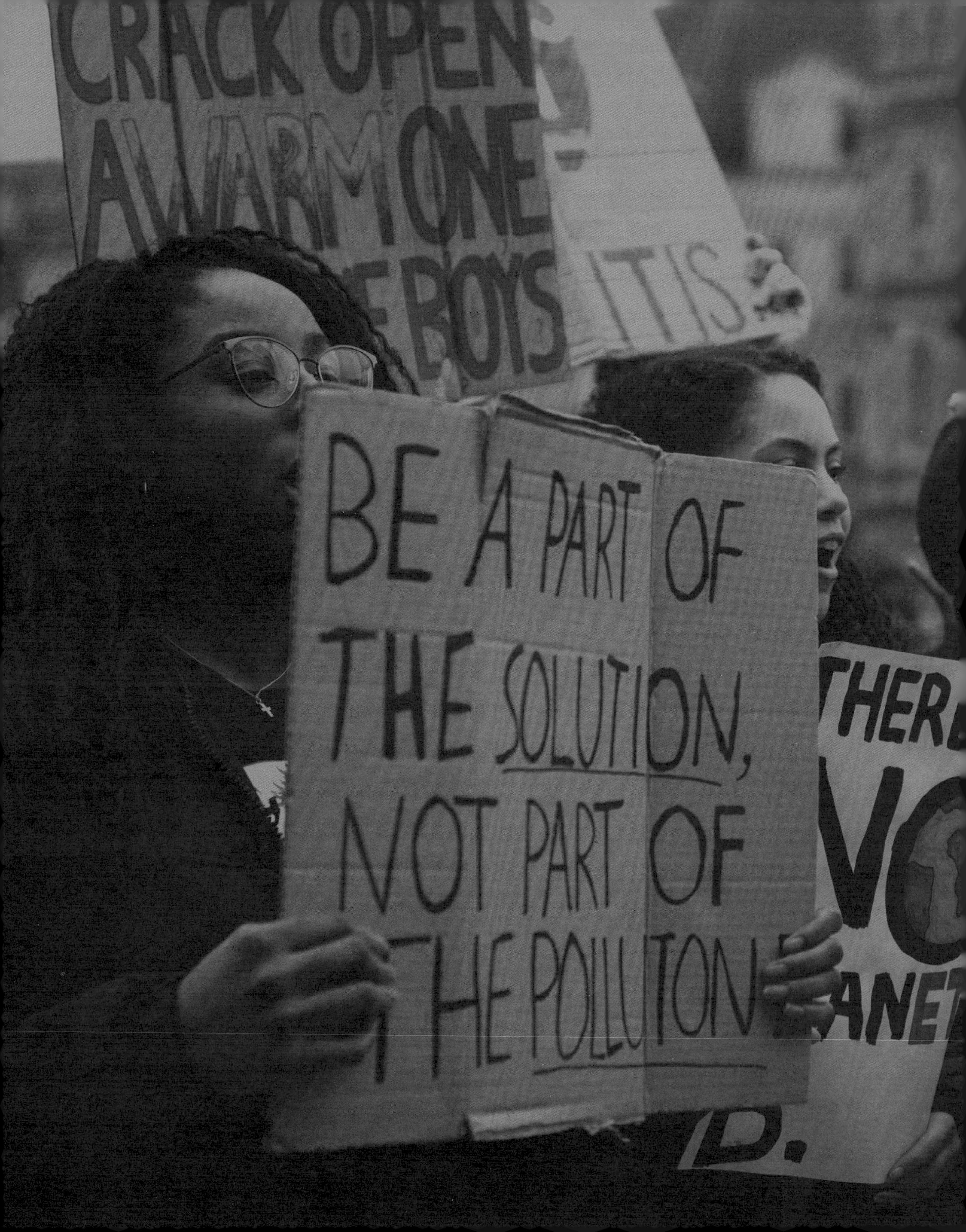
CRACK OPEN
A WARM ONE
BE A PART OF
THE SOLUTION,
NOT PART OF

Global climate protests have increased significantly over the past few years, with high profile actors such as Extinction Rebellion and Greta Thunberg bringing political and media attention to the issue.

Architecture and the Climate Emergency

Editor's Note

2019 was a year of great change in the world of climate awareness, with the rise of environmental activists such as Greta Thunberg and Extinction Rebellion speaking against a backdrop of unprecedented heatwaves, wildfires, flooding and storms. 2020 drew the debate into even sharper focus with the COVID-19 pandemic showing us the fragility and inequality of our current system. The 'extractivist' age is drawing to a close, and we are on the brink of a paradigm shift that will affect the way in which we interact with the world around us.

Every minute of the day we pollute rivers and the air we breathe and we use resources we can never again replenish. We live in a world where we burn dirty fuels that are now unbearably heating up the very planet that has been sheltering and nurturing humans and other species for millions of years. Typically, each architecture project has contributed to the problem. Instead, every architecture project needs to lead us towards the sustainable tomorrow we want and need.

In response to these issues, and for the first RIBA Design Studio, we have put together a special volume that focuses on how we can find solutions to the current climatic, environmental and social challenges that we face together. We have compiled a collection of articles written by, and in conversation with, inspirational and committed architects, educators and students who are – in their own way, and in different ways – working to make a difference in architecture at the coalface of climate change.

With no exception, they are working tirelessly and creatively to highlight the fact that beauty, delight and architectural quality go hand in hand to build a positive future.

From climate change to climate crisis and the climate and ecological emergency

On a global scale we must significantly reduce the burning of fossil fuels now to prevent run-away climate change, and we have perhaps less than a decade to transition towards a carbon neutral society.[1] We are also using resources at a rate that they cannot be replenished. Our individual and collective actions are irreparably damaging nature, leading to species' decline and extinctions.[2]

Architects are – finally – starting to 'get it'. The science and the facts speak for themselves about the impact architects have: the design and construction of buildings uses around 40% of the EU's energy and is responsible for around 36% of CO2 emissions,[3] significantly contributing to the current climate crisis.

Sofie Pelsmakers and Nick Newman

Extinction Rebellion floating a model house down the River Thames in 2019, as a protest against rising sea levels.

Decisively, architects, students and educators declared a biodiversity and climate emergency, with a global 'call for change' to respond to climatic and ecological challenges, both in practice and in the education of future architects.

System change not climate change

Tom Bennett from Studio Bark in the UK argues in his thought-provoking article that for the first time mainstream commentators are acknowledging the possibility of full-scale civilisational collapse. Faced with a problem so systemic and so urgent in our way of collective living, it seems rather hubristic that we may be able to 'architect our way out of the problem' by making incremental design choices. Danish architect Dorte Mandrup recognises that no easy solutions exist and that countries need to set regulatory pressures to achieve the needed systemic shift, while Professor Kongjian Yu from Turenscape in China campaigns to persuade local decision-makers to do things differently.

The question arises of what architecture is, and if it must involve building from new or building at all. This theme features in several pieces, including one from Kari Kytölä, Paulina Sawczuk and Satu Huuhka in Finland, who explore material resources and argue to 'rethink, think twice, and think ahead', challenging architects to change their wasteful practices. Anders Lendager is doing exactly that in Denmark, challenging business as usual by using waste as new building materials, and changing design and building processes as a result. Mario Kolkwitz and Elina Luotonen further argue for a shift in thinking and practice in conversation with raumlabor in Berlin and Al Borde in Ecuador.

How much systemic change can be achieved in architecture when the world around us continues with business as usual? When we work on projects that promote infinite growth, while this is incompatible with a sustainable world, how much can we really influence? If architects are unable to make changes within the system, they need to change the system.

Mikhail Riches show some powerful impacts designers can make by showing what they will not do. The practice profile highlights the brave decision to put its head above the parapet and publicly refuse to work on projects that do not meet its values. While not all architects might be in a position to do this, if our clients and overheads do not permit us to make radical changes to the status quo alone, we must come together through movements such as Architects Declare and Architects Climate Action Network to demand systemic change from those in power.

It is not just architectural practice but also architectural education that needs a systemic shift. The ACAN Education group highlights that architects need knowledge and competencies which are not currently being taught to students. Nevertheless, seeing student projects infuses us with hope; educators Kasia Nawratek at Manchester Metropolitan University in the UK, and Elizabeth Donovan, Urszula Kozminska, Nacho Ruiz Allen and Thomas R. Hilberth at the Aarhus School of Architecture (AAA) in Denmark all exemplify their educational practices with student projects that integrate climatic and ecological issues in a creative and inspirational way.

Share your resources

To be a part of systemic change, we can no longer entertain the traditional view of the architect who designs and builds alone. We must build on each other's ideas, encouragement, knowledge and, most importantly, expertise. We have neither the time nor the resources to waste or to get it wrong.

All the contributions in this volume highlight that real change was only achieved through collaboration within and outside architecture as a discipline, including working with the people and communities for whom we design. Indeed, this is the modus operandi of practices such as raumlabor and Al Borde. In Norway, at Helen & Hard, some of the architects have even taken up residence in their co-produced, ground-breaking, co-living housing scheme.

We also need to be resourceful in other ways. In Anyana Zimmermann and Fabián Rodríguez Izquierdo's reflective account of Cuban adaptability, they challenge architects to 'think like a Cuban and design like you are in an embargo', and use materials as sparingly and resourcefully as Cubans have had to do over several decades of economic and climate related hardships. Hiroshi Sambuichi, in conversation with Professor Andrew Barrie, also inspires us not to forget about the natural resources around us, and to use 'moving materials' such as air, light and heat to 'construct' buildings.

Zimmermann and Rodríguez Izquierdo also argue for future-thinking, because we are already facing unprecedented climatic shifts. Global heating affects how we live, design and build, as echoed by Sambuichi in seeing natural conditions change over time. So, we must design in adaptive measures today, learning lessons from other parts of the world. Some student projects at AAA show how this is done at the education level, using climatic change as the foundation of their work and a generator of their design and creativity.

Architecture that mends

Once we have found the courage to change our collective consciousness, what can we do to help rebuild the world we have spent so long destroying?

Professor Kongjian Yu at Turenscape shows us how to think about our cities on the scale of an ecosystem and implement huge landscape regeneration programmes which are as beautiful as they are healing and resilient to future climate changes. In Australia, Stephen Choi shows us a holistic approach to think about buildings as 'living' and incorporate so much more than just shelter and comfort when we plan them; weaving together energy, access to nature, human scale, health and well-being, careful use and consideration of material, water resources and waste, as well as responding to issues of equity where anyone in the community – rather than just the affluent – can be part of the project.

Global citizens

We are global citizens. The things we do affect the climate, resources and quality of environment and life thousands of miles away and vice versa. Yet, it is often forgotten in architectural practice. Materials are often specified from other countries because it is cheaper, but this ignores the cost to the environment from shipping goods halfway across the world. It also ignores the cost of less stringent environmental controls that affects people and environments, or the political regimes our purchasing power unintentionally support. The same system encourages us to import biofuels from far away, despite rainforest being cleared to grow these crops, and people losing their livelihoods and ability to feed themselves, so we can heat our buildings while forests burn and land erodes and floods.

While a globalised world makes this possible, it has also connected us as people closer together and given us many opportunities; but architects can no longer take the benefits of a globalised world and ignore the consequences and climate injustices. Our global membership comes with great responsibility and should not be left at the door of the architect's office.

Finally, as global citizens ourselves, we sought to broaden out the discussion of this volume from a European-centric narrative and include voices of change from different socio-economic and geographic locations and communities. We see beautiful and thoughtful work from SRDA's poetic piece on school building in India with a call for architects to empower students in creativity, alongside dRMM's Kingsdale School which includes a retrofit and new low-impact building in a disadvantaged London neighbourhood.

There are countless other architects and projects outside this volume that we encourage you to research and draw inspiration from, including Francis Kere's meticulously detailed low-impact schools in Gando, and Atelier Masomi in Niger, with its 'designs that sustain people' mapped around a concern for human rights, the climate and local culture. Likewise, Shigeru Ban's quiet approach to sustainability and where they might go next, or RotorDC's building deconstruction facility in Belgium.

While we cannot provide a definitive outlook on the subject, we ask all designers and students to consider and invite as many voices into the discussion whilst you continue your own work. Diversity brings different viewpoints that we need more than ever, because the same people that created, benefited from and upheld the current extractive system are unlikely to be the ones to change it. In acting together, we can achieve the systemic change we urgently need. We challenge you to join us on this journey and to make a difference in your own work for a more sustainable and equitable tomorrow.

1 https://www.ipcc.ch/sr15/
2 https://www.un.org/sustainabledevelopment/blog/2019/05/nature-decline-unprecedented-report/
3 EC (2019), 'New rules for greener and smarter buildings will increase quality of life for all Europeans', https://ec.europa.eu/info/news/new-rules-greener-and-smarter-buildings-will-increase-quality-life-all-europeans-2019-apr-15_en

Dorte Mandrup Arkitekter, Ilulissat Icefjord Centre, Ilulissat, Greenland, completion expected 2021. Steel and timber construction based on local conditions, ensuring sustainable solutions suited to the context. Renders by MIR.

Creating Change with Impact: An Architect's Manifesto

Dorte Mandrup

If we do not change our behaviour radically, we will reach a point of irreversible damage to our planet within the next 12 years.

Architects across the globe must acknowledge that evidence and contextual understanding is key to sustainable design. Knowledge and skills within architecture and education need to be broadened and deepened. We need to share best practices and dare to experiment to find sustainable solutions that are more than buzzwords and good intentions.

In 2018, the world's leading climate scientists warned that: if we do not change our behaviour radically, we will reach a point of irreversible damage to our planet by 2030. In the Intergovernmental Panel on Climate Change's (IPCC's) Special Report, the dire reality of global warming is outlined and the now well-known 1.5 °C target is set.[1] The report warns that exceeding this level of global warming by even half a degree will have catastrophic consequences, as it will significantly worsen the risks of drought, floods, extreme heat and poverty for hundreds of millions of people.

To avoid such irreversible damage, the report concludes that we must make 'rapid, far-reaching and unprecedented changes in all aspects of society'.[2]

The following years have been spent discussing this new reality and possible ways of staying within the targeted 1.5°C. To do so, global greenhouse gas emissions must be reduced by 45% by 2030, reaching net zero by 2050. The built environment as an industry is responsible for almost 40% of global energy related emissions. Architects of today and tomorrow are in a unique position to create change with significant impact and must find ways of radical improvement. It is crucial that the knowledge and skills needed to design buildings without compromising the opportunities of future generations are acquired.

And it must be done now.

Call for political action

On both a local and global scale, there are a number of positive initiatives slowly moving in the right direction. Many are exploring the potentials of building in timber or reusing construction materials. However, the green transitioning in the building sector is nowhere near the necessary pace of development – especially considering the rate of new construction. It is expected that the global building stock will double as the world's population approaches 10 billion in 2050. In observing the actual changes in the building sector over the last

couple of years, it is evident that the free market neither has the ability nor the willingness to transition at the required pace.

Political action is necessary to create requirements and incentives that speed up behavioural change and motivate innovation. It is crucial for governments across the globe to step in and force all industries, including the building industry, to adapt to this urgent ecological crisis and make sustainable construction not only a priority but also a requirement.

In Denmark, it is demonstrated how political action can be a powerful tool to accelerate green transitioning. Since the oil crisis of the 1970s, the Danish government has worked consistently to find alternative sources of energy supply.[3] As a result, the building industry has been forced to discuss different ways of reducing energy consumption. Decades of ambitious requirements and incentives have forced both public and private stakeholders to upscale and innovate.

Following a long tradition of calculating cost per square metre in financial terms, Danish architectural practices have now become comfortable measuring energy consumption in kilowatt hours per square

Dorte Mandrup Arkitekter, Ilulissat Icefjord Centre, Ilulissat, Greenland, completion expected 2021. The aerodynamic form reduces snow build-up while framing views towards the Icefjord.

metre, and all new buildings in Denmark are allowed a maximum of 40 kilowatt hours per square metre per year (kWh/m²a). Coupled with a political push for energy renovations of the older building stock and an overall tightened code, Denmark is today at the forefront when it comes to reducing building energy use.

Globally, operational carbon emissions (i.e. the CO_2 emissions associated with building energy use) make up 28% of the well-known 40% total carbon emissions impact from buildings, whereas the remaining 11% comes from materials and construction impacts.[4] So, knowledge about how to build energy efficiently is extremely important for the green transitioning in the building industry.

However, it is not the solution to have tunnel vision on just one aspect of sustainability. Attention must be turned to materials, evidence and context. As buildings become increasingly energy efficient, emissions related to construction and materials will become proportionately larger. Therefore, it is crucial to start talking about how to minimise the overall environmental footprint of a building, considering operational emissions and emissions related to construction and materials, and other associated impacts on factors such as health biodiversity, waste.

The global climate goals can only be achieved if everyone works together. If we can export knowledge from countries such as Denmark to other countries, and learn from others, there is an opportunity for all of us to move forward, so that together we can find a common approach to holistic sustainability.

Using evidence and understanding materials in context

In its essence, sustainability is a science. It cannot be only engineers and other specialists finding green solutions for designs – sustainability needs to be an integral part of the architectural design process. If equipped with evidence, architects are in a unique position to incorporate sustainability into all aspects of a building's lifetime.

Many methods, tools and certifications have been or are currently being developed to go beyond kilowatt per square metre towards a language of an environmental footprint per square metre. However, the current certifications are often too focused on operational emissions.

Sustainable architecture is context-dependent. For example, several factors make up the environmental footprint of wood in a specific context, such as the typical need for impregnation, durability under the specific climatic conditions, availability of wood in the local area and problems of deforestation. What is needed is cradle-to-cradle tools, such as Life Cycle Assessment (LCA), that look holistically at the sustainability profile of a building and take all associated impacts into account. This starts from the extraction of raw materials and the use of natural resources to the production of materials and construction of building, to use, renovation and end-of-life with demolition, disposal, and re-/upcycling. By holistically assessing all parameters of a building's lifecycle, we obtain data about a variety of different choices, which gives us the power to make informed design decisions. Only equipped with evidence

It cannot be only engineers and other specialists finding green solutions for designs – sustainability needs to be an integral part of the architectural design process.

Dorte Mandrup
Arkitekter, Wadden Sea
Centre, Ribe, Denmark,
2017. The building is an
interpretation of local
building traditions and
rural farmhouse typology
significant in the area.

is it possible to decrease the overall environmental footprint of a building.

Without evidence, well-meaning sustainability initiatives can in fact lead to increased overall emissions. Implementing a tool like LCA as an integrated part of our design process, end-to-end plays a vital role in upskilling and educating architects and clients alike. Being a relatively new tool for measuring environmental impact, it is still a challenge to define the standards and methods of LCA:

· how long building components should be considered
· expected lifetimes of specific materials
· how to take account of sources of renewable energy
  have been topics of discussion.

Collectively, the construction industry has a responsibility to collect the evidence necessary for upgrading the global industry's knowledge on buildings' environmental impact. Shared documentation and results make assessing a building's footprint easier each time.

Evidence in practice

In 2016, Dorte Mandrup won the competition to design a project for the Ilulissat Icefjord Centre 250 km north of the Arctic Circle in Greenland, which truly demonstrates the complexity of a building's environmental footprint. There is a lack of building materials in Greenland and therefore all materials are imported. As a result, a central consideration in the design process has been the weight of the materials and the ability to pack them efficiently.

Initially, it was intended to be a timber construction for the environmental benefits of wood, amongst other reasons. However, one of the consequences of climate change in a Greenlandic context is a prolonged period where the weather shifts between thaw and frost before turning to a stable state for a longer period, which has an impact on how materials, including wood, react and behave over time. Studies show that for it to be a durable solution in these conditions, the components of wood had to be very large and heavy. In this context, the environmental benefits of a timber construction would not have outweighed the environmental costs of transportation or a shortened lifespan of the building. As a result, some of the construction was changed to steel, ensuring the durability of the building and minimising the overall environmental impact.

In the same fashion, choosing reeds as the dominant material in the transformation and extension of the Wadden Sea Centre was a logical choice because of the possibility of harvesting high-quality reeds in

Dorte Mandrup Arkitekter, Wadden Sea Centre, Ribe, Denmark, 2017. 25,000 bundles of thatching reeds harvested in the local area were used for the building.

the local area. Not only are emissions related to transportation minimised, but some also argue that the reeds will perform better in their own environment in terms of fungi and overall durability. This is an area where more research is needed to document how reeds grown in different places perform in their local environment as compared to being used in other weather conditions and climates, highlighting that sustainable solutions in one project are not necessarily sustainable in others.

It is crucial to make informed choices and to analyse the limitations and potentials of materials under very specific conditions. Truly understanding the qualities of a material at a given site is not necessarily a quick exercise.

Similarly, it requires revisiting a work and studying how, and if, it performs as intended; not only after one and five years after but also 10, 20 and even 50 years down the line. To avoid repeating mistakes, long-term evaluation needs to be prioritised and made an integrated practice.

Architecting in a world of scarce resources

Architects and students are also existing in a world with scarce resources. Every time something new is built, it is necessary to ask whether it is the most environmentally, economically and socially efficient way of utilising our common resources.

Reusing and recycling materials can have a significant effect on reducing carbon emissions by minimising waste and reducing the need for new materials. Viewing the built environment as a material bank, it holds a vast amount of resources and aesthetic qualities perfectly good for reuse. Developing better methods of converting materials is a central part of green transitioning to meet our emission targets. In the UK, it is estimated that 80% of the buildings that will exist in 2050 have already been constructed. This emphasises the importance of decarbonising the existing building stock and prioritising transformations, as only so much progress can be made by concentrating on the efficiency and construction of new buildings.

When solving an architectural task which includes an obsolete building, the first thing should be to investigate the potentials of what is already there. Is it possible and viable to transform the existing structure? Which materials can be reused in the construction of a new building? How can the upcycling process be executed locally? Does the old structure or materials hold any aesthetic value? This requires a new

Dorte Mandrup Arkitekter, Wadden Sea Centre, Ribe, Denmark, 2017. The thatched roofs and facades underline the tactile qualities and robustness that can be found in traditional crafts and materials of the region.

mindset for all stakeholders along the value chain to search for potentials rather than obstacles.

As Chair of the Mies van der Rohe Award jury in 2019, I had the pleasure of visiting an unconventional project demonstrating the architectural potentials of a series of homogeneous, concrete social housing blocks from the 1960s. We granted Europe's most powerful architecture prize to our French colleagues Lacaton & Vassal for the transformation of the 530-dwelling Grand Parc Bordeaux. Instead of demolishing the decaying housing blocks and forcing people out of their homes, the blocks have been refurbished by adding an external layer of winter gardens and balconies. The original facades have been removed and the apartments have been opened up to light, air and views. Despite a low budget the architects have managed to add not only square metres but also true architectural value to each housing unit without having to relocate the residents during construction. Hopefully, the project will inspire future renovations of the many, many dwellings built in the 1960s and '70s throughout Europe.

The same mindset is needed when deciding that the best thing is to build new. Large parts of the current building stock have been built with no regard for the fact that society and the needs for the built environment are constantly changing. For the benefit of future generations of architects, we must design architecture that can be transformed, reused and upcycled. So many resources go to waste when buildings are designed only for the future that we know and can predict, with materials that cannot be reused and structures not strong enough to carry alterations. Therefore, architects of today and tomorrow, make the choice to transform your building rather than tearing it down, create architecture that can be altered and re-imagined to fit different needs, and create strong structures that can be taken apart and upcycled for new and unknown purposes.

Without experiments, no change

To achieve the necessary changes in architecture to help reach the 2030 and 2050 European CO2 Reduction targets requires experimentation and an acceptance of the associated risks of doing something new. A failed experiment offers findings and experience on which to base the next experiment.

Test the unknown with the courage to challenge those sticking to conformity. Dare to experiment, knowing that experiments do not always succeed.

When approaching a unique landscape, such

Dorte Mandrup Arkitekter, Trilateral Wadden Sea World Heritage Partnership Centre, Wilhelmshaven, Germany, ongoing. The Trilateral Wadden Sea World Heritage Partnership Centre will use as little land and resources as possible by sitting cantilevered atop an existing bunker.

Dorte Mandrup Arkitekter, Trilateral Wadden Sea World Heritage Partnership Centre, Wilhelmshaven, Germany, ongoing. The bunker will be used for exhibition space and its roof will be reinvented into an internal courtyard, ensuring daylight throughout the building.

Architecture and the Climate Emergency

Dorte Mandrup Arkitekter, Sundbyøster Hall II, Copenhagen, Denmark, 2015. After nightfall, the pleated red-golden wooden facade will appear to be glowing due to the escaping lights from the vertical ribbon windows reflecting on the warm tinted wood.

Test the unknown with the courage to challenge those sticking to conformity.

Dorte Mandrup Arkitekter, Sundbyøster Hall II, Copenhagen, Denmark, 2015. With a supermarket on the ground floor, a sports hall on the first floor and apartments with private atrium terraces on the top floor, Sundbyøster Hall II is an architectural three-in-one solution.

as the marshlands by the Wadden Sea where strong winds and a saline climate sets the agenda for the architecture, it is relevant to look towards the local building traditions and craftsmanship that have survived there for hundreds of years. Process it, challenge it, experiment with it, reinterpret it and make it your own. Pay homage to its robust qualities but test its boundaries and ask the 'what-ifs'. What if we not only use water reeds as roofing, but also create a large sculptural overhang and facades coated in water reeds?

When a historic bunker from the Second World War sits on-site and creates a natural anchoring point in an otherwise open field, look for its architectural potentials rather than how to remove or build around it, as we did in Wilhelmshaven, Germany. What if the heavy bunker is actually an opportunity to use as little land and resources as possible? What if the building has the bunker as its robust foundation, and thereby contributes to preserve an agonising but historic wartime relic, while holding a unique aesthetic quality?

When designing a sports hall in a complex urban environment with a desperate need for more housing, test the boundaries of a sports hall. What if you can build apartments on top and a supermarket at ground level? What if a sports hall can become an architectural three-in-one solution serving several needs of the city while saving space and resources in a dense urban district?

It takes a lot of courage not to just go with the flow and take the easy way out. Future generations of politicians, city planners, architects, developers and manufacturers must be courageous.

Without experiments, there will be no change.

Architects of tomorrow: take the lead

So, architects of tomorrow, advance your toolbox, deepen your knowledge and equip yourself with evidence. Do not settle for a singular solution to sustainable architecture but insist on making solutions based on context-specific choices. Keep exploring and challenging the field of architecture and dare to experiment, because radical changes and new ideas are necessary for reaching the 2050 target.

Finally, take the lead on sustainably sound developments to ensure that sustainability will never become an argument for bad architecture.

1 'Global Warming of 1.5°C', Intergovernmental Panel on Climate Change, 2020, https://www.ipcc.ch/sr15/
2 Ibid.
3 Rüdiger, M., 'Den fossile kultur og oliekriserne', Danmarks Historien, 2019, https://danmarkshistorien.dk/leksikon-og-kilder/vis/materiale/den-fossile-kultur-og-oliekriserne/
4 'Bringing Embodied Carbon Upfront', World Green Building Council, 2019, https://www.worldgbc.org/embodied-carbon

Not Opposites:
A Conversation with
Hiroshi Sambuichi on
Architecture and Nature

Andrew Barrie

From his earliest days, Hiroshi Sambuichi's work has been characterised by astonishing design discipline and care for the resources used in its creation. An early project built of in-situ concrete was cast in specially designed wooden formwork panels carefully sized and detailed to allow their re-use as doors and sections of flooring.

As the years have passed, this ecological concern expanded into a conception of architecture in which Sambuichi manipulates air, water and sunlight as 'moving materials'. Using the heat of the sun or cool water from underground, flows of air and moisture are composed and detailed as integral and often fundamental elements of Sambuichi's buildings. His projects often involve long periods of research to understand the history of their sites, the surrounding topography and wind and weather patterns. Likewise, the design process involves careful experimentation with models and prototypes to study and refine airflows, porosities to light and wind, material choices and other aspects of his buildings.

In February 2020, Sambuichi and his young family visited New Zealand at the invitation of Soichiro Fukutake, who has been a key supporter of his work. Fukutake, who now lives in Auckland but was the driving force behind the 'art islands' in Japan's Seto Inland Sea, was the patron of Sambuichi's projects on the islands of Inujima and Naoshima. Andrew Barrie spoke to Sambuichi about these projects and others located around the Seto.

Andrew Barrie: Your work is best known for symbiosis between architecture and nature, focusing on what you call 'moving materials'. Can you start by explaining this?
Hiroshi Sambuichi: Architecture is a part of the earth. We usually suppose construction materials are things that don't move, such as concrete and wood, but moving materials like air, wind, water and sun are important. Maybe we don't think enough about the relationship between air and water. People might think that water is heavier than air, but the power of the sun turns water into mist and then it cools into rain. The water becomes lighter and then heavier again; this is the earth's cycle. We pay attention to these moving materials when they come into contact with the earth. If they move too fast, they're very dangerous.

AB: A storm is air moving too fast.
A flood is water moving too fast.
HS: Yes, so changing their speed is important. Such change is something we can do with architecture.
AB: You grew up in the city of Hiroshima, located on the shores of the Seto Inland Sea, with its many islands. It sits in a very dramatic landscape. What made it a special place to be raised?
HS: I was born not far from Miyajima Island, where the Itsukushima Shrine is located. It is a beautiful example of architecture that takes moving materials into account. Miyajima is an island of the gods, and it's also an island of moving materials. Itsukushima Shrine is a UNESCO World Heritage site and uses the tides beautifully; it brings the moon, landform and water into play. The most important event there is the Kangeisai Festival, which happens on the day of the full moon. It starts at low tide, and as the moon rises so does the tide. At high tide you can ride a boat through the gate to the shrine to pray, which has been the route to prayer for 1,000 years. It means you can't just go when you like, but only when the tides are right. It's the moon that decides when you visit. The form of the shrine itself was also decided by moving materials. It sits out over the water, with the level of its raised floor decided by nature so that it won't be carried away by the tides, making it similar to a mangrove tree. The shrine has become one with its natural surroundings.

Visitors to Miyajima often climb up 500 m to a mountain peak, and you can see the message of moving materials as you go up. At the base of the slope you can see fir trees, which grew after a landslide, giving us the message: 'Don't build here.' They look after us. At around 300 m you can see moss, which tells us that there is a lot of water vapour and mist. At the top, you can see bare rocks, which shows how severe nature can be.

The peak was a place of pilgrimage, called an iwakura, and it is said the gods sit on the stones. From there, you can look over Japan's Seto Inland Sea; it's a beautiful panorama.

I designed the Mount Misen Observatory, where you can witness the moving materials. It's called za, which means 'to sit down', although the meaning is a little more complex. The idea of sitting and appreciating the natural world has been handed down through the generations and I wanted to bring that into the observatory. For roughly the last 100 years, people have been trying to control nature. In Japan we have a culture of working with nature to create architecture. In designing this observatory, I wanted to go back to

Sambuichi Architects, Miyajima Misen Observatory, Miyajima Island, Japan, 2013. This project is located 500 m above sea level at the summit of Mount Misen. Accessed by ropeways and hiking trails, the peak is a venerated Buddhist pilgrimage site and offers spectacular views over the islands of the Seto Inland Sea.

For roughly the last 100 years, people have been trying to control nature. In Japan we have a culture of working with nature to create architecture.

Itsukushima Shrine, Miyajima Island, Japan, twelfth century. Regarded as one of Japan's most scenic spots, this shrine stands at the base of steep hills and looks across the ocean to the city of Hiroshima. The Miyajima Misen Observatory stands at the peak of those hills.

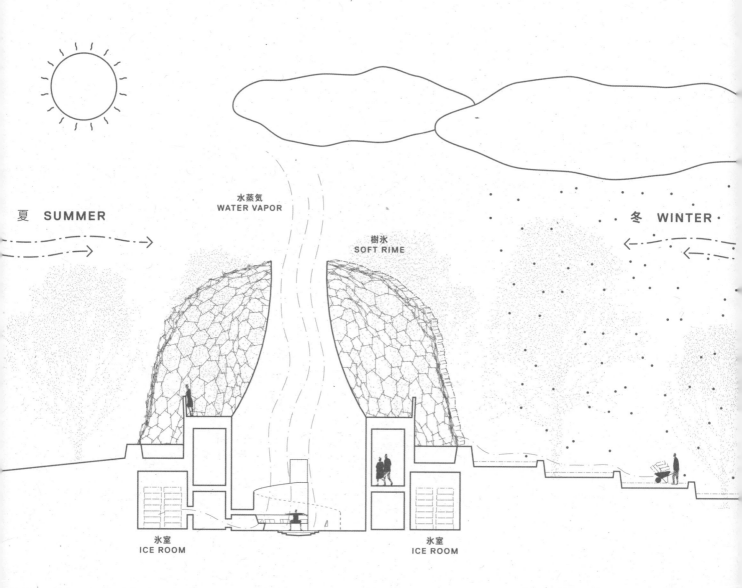

Sambuichi Architects, Rokko Shidare Observatory, Kobe, Japan, 2010. Ponds that in summer serve as reflecting pools, in winter serve as a source of ice. Cut into blocks, this ice is in placed in insulated storage rooms and serves as a natural source of cooling for the rest of the year.

夏 SUMMER

水蒸気
WATER VAPOR

樹氷
SOFT RIME

冬 WINTER

氷室
ICE ROOM

氷室
ICE ROOM

the way we thought 1,000 years ago, when we sat and worshipped nature. I really like the fact that everyone here in New Zealand wants to look after nature. In Japan, as well, we have a culture of working with nature to create architecture.

Sitting is very important. You can sit on all sides of the observatory and the view is from a very low angle, where you can see the rocks where the gods were said to sit and revere nature. The sunshade was designed low, so if you're standing you can't see out, which means you have to sit down. It allows you to look and really see those moving materials in motion. You can see the sun changing the mist into clouds and it becomes even more beautiful; nature and architecture become one. Itsukushima Shrine is a good example, where you can see nature and its movements more clearly because of the building. If it wasn't there, I don't think you'd be able to see the tides as easily.

The role of architecture is to show us nature.

AB: This project on Mount Misen wasn't your first observatory, as you'd already designed the Rokko Shidare Observatory at the opposite end of the Seto Inland Sea. What made your first project different?

HS: The site on Mount Rokko is at a height of 1,000 m above sea level, so you can look out over Kobe and Osaka. This project resulted from a competition and, whilst all the other proposals were for looking at the city views at night, I wanted to make a place where you could see nature.

At that altitude you get very particular movements of nature. I discovered that they had particularly beautiful hoar frost, so I wanted to make an observatory where you could see it. The hoar frost occurs in some spots and not others, which requires 100% humidity, a temperature of minus five degrees, and a wind speed of about 5 m per second. To figure out how to promote the frost forming, I did some experiments with wooden poles, making ten different prototypes, varying the spacing of the poles, how thick they were, and so on.

The hoar frost forms on a mesh on the outside of the observatory. Inside, I created a chimney and on the slopes around arranged shallow ponds. You don't need a river, and there is no well; the sun brings water up to this altitude as mist. In winter, it freezes into ice and we take that ice and store it in insulated storerooms. In summer it melts, creating cool air that is pulled out by the natural power of the chimney. People inside can feel cool air coming out of armrests in the seats; in these moments, it allows you to feel the earth turning.

The air creates hoar frost on the mesh, the sun melts it and the water flows back down the mountain.

We completed the building ten years ago. At that time, the ice was 20 cm thick, but last year it was just 8 cm. In the winter of 2020, there wasn't even 1 cm of ice, so you can feel how quickly global warming is advancing.

People think of architecture and nature as being opposites or contrasting, whereas I believe these projects show that we can make something beautiful if we work with nature, and within it.

AB: About 15 years ago you were asked by Soichiro Fukutake to design the Inujima Seirensho Art Museum on the island of Inujima. Repairing damage was central to the project. Could you explain the process?

HS: This region had minerals, so they were mined and a copper refinery was built on the island. The pollution from the refinery caused all the plants to die. It was a place where nature had been destroyed. I was asked to bring life back to the island through architecture. When I first went to Inujima with Mr Fukutake, I saw villagers living on part of the island, but elsewhere there were just the ruins and old chimneys of the refinery. There were lots of black bricks, looking like they'd just been thrown away, which had been made from what was left over after the copper was extracted.

To start the renewal, I began research and focused on those black bricks. Even in winter, they are very warm to the touch, so I thought I could use them to collect heat from the sun. I always ended up at a chimney when I explored the refinery ruins, where you could feel really cool air being drawn through and upwards, and it gave me the idea of using the chimney for cooling. We could use the sun to make air warmer and lighter and use the existing chimney to pull that air through the building. It was possible to create an art gallery that didn't need air conditioning. I also thought about the entrance; where would the air come in? Usually an art gallery has an entry for people but this one has two: one for people and one for air. When I showed my idea to Mr Fukutake, he immediately understood and agreed to proceed. It was a very exciting project.

AB: You created a room with a glass roof and a floor of the black bricks, which warms up even in winter. You don't reach this room until the end of the visit, but it's located next to the entry. By opening and closing doors, you can change the source of the air being drawn through the building. In summer it's cooler air from outside, and in winter it's warm air from the glazed room. What was the idea behind it?

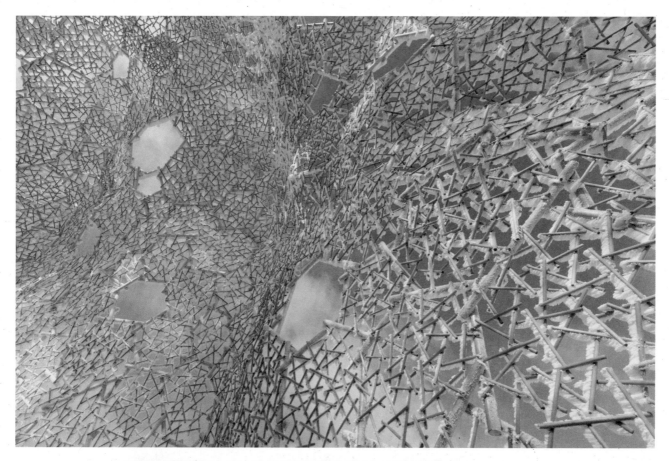

Sambuichi Architects, Rokko Shidare Observatory, Kobe, Japan, 2010. Located on a high ridge overlooking the city of Kobe, this project has extensive views over the cityscapes and islands arranged around Osaka Bay.

Architecture and the Climate Emergency

HS: As long as the sun keeps rising, it will keep happening. So, if an 80 year-old villager opens the door in the morning, the air will flow and the art gallery can open. You don't need any buttons, computers or anything else. To run this place, you just open the door.

Mr Fukutake's message is: 'Use what exists to create what is to be.' It's a wonderful message that means there's no need to hurry, you need to think about what's there. You also need to think about the air, the sun, the wind and about the things that have been thrown away, like those bricks. If you use what's there to make something new, it's something that can't be imitated elsewhere. Usually people want to make new things by bringing stuff from somewhere else, but using what's there means that you can make architecture that could exist only there.

AB: It's very unusual to have a client that is willing to let you take the time needed to develop such solutions. Can you use this way of working under other circumstances?

HS: I've also used this method on a different island – Naoshima. I started on the Naoshima Plan with Mr Fukutake in 2011. Naoshima is renowned for modern art and modern architecture, but it's also a place for moving materials, particularly the circulation of air and water on the island.

I like research, history and landforms. I like looking at how people live in various places. People began living on Naoshima thousands of years ago and about 400 years ago they started building a town. Studying the town now, you can see that they carefully considered how water moved, creating a grid of water channels and the considering the layout of the houses. On the islands of the Seto Inland Sea, the houses were usually built side-by-side, but on Naoshima they were separate, each with their own gate and garden. I discovered that these houses were laid out with the direction of the wind in mind. The wind blows from the south, and the houses all had living rooms that the wind could pass straight through. The air moved from house to house, through one and then the next like passing a baton in a relay. It's a beautiful way of thinking about a whole town, rather than thinking just about yourself or your own house. Looking not only at the layout of the village but also the landscape, I discovered that the rice paddies had also been laid out with the direction of the wind in mind. In summer, the rice paddies are full of water and it becomes cool as the wind passes over them, and then this cool air flows into the houses in the village. Both the landscape and houses were designed with moving materials in mind.

Back in the Edo Period (1603–1868), they had wells under the houses too, so that every house in the village could bring up about two tons of water a day for washing, drinking and cooking. The water is about 15 degrees when it comes up and must have cooled down the villagers. The water would then to go back into the ground, cool down and eventually be drawn back up. These days, they have lots of asphalt and everything feels hotter because of it. The water the villagers use in their houses goes out to sea, up to the clouds and eventually comes back down with the water circulating above ground.

We're making new things on Naoshima, thinking about this circulation of water. We went back to thinking about how we could use that cool ground water that's no longer being drawn on. We've completed a project, called 'The Water', which uses well water. It's a renovation of a 200-year-old building that was a post office with gardens on the north and south sides, creating a route for the wind.

AB: You've inserted a shallow pond, and the running well fills the building with the sounds of water, which psychologically has a cooling effect.

HS: In the Naoshima Plan, now we are making a lot of different houses that use water. It could suddenly get very cool on Naoshima as we use that water from below [laughs].

Architecture can be thought of as a letter to the future. All those years ago, they built buildings that used water from below ground and relayed air through the village. I took on board that message from 400 years ago and brought it forward to make the villagers something new. So, I'm thinking of people 400 years from now and what message I should send them. That's how I come up with the things you see in my architecture; by taking that letter from the past and thinking about what to write to the future.

AB: Returning to Hiroshima, one of the interesting things about it as a city is simply that it isn't Tokyo or Osaka. Has living and working there been important in the development of your thinking?

HS: Hiroshima is a city of moving materials because of the Seto Inland Sea and the mountains on either side. Around Hiroshima, about 90% of the land area is forest, 4% is rice paddies and fields, and the remaining 6% is the town. About 400 years ago, a town was created beside a river and a castle was placed at its centre.

Sambuichi Architects, Inujima Seirensho Museum, Inujima Island, Japan, 2008. Designed by Hiroshi Sambuichi, this museum is operated by the Fukutake Foundation with artwork by Yukinori Yanagi. Inserted into the remnants of a long-abandoned copper refinery, it was slotted in among ruined storage bays formed from the black bricks of slag left over after the refining process.

Architecture can be thought of as a letter to the future

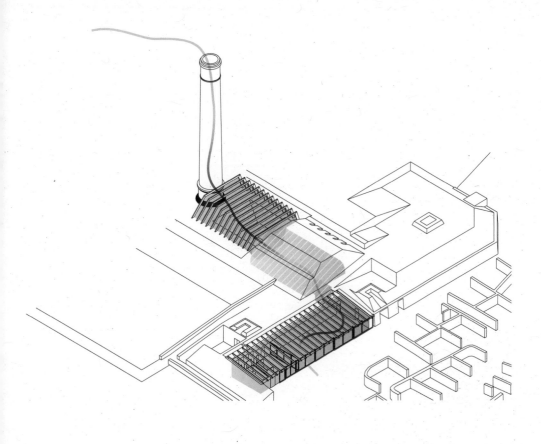

Left: Sambuichi Architects, Inujima Seirensho Museum, Inujima Island, Japan, 2008. In winter, air is warmed in a glazed gallery and then drawn into the main museum chamber (above); in summer, air is cooled as it passes through an underground passage. (below)

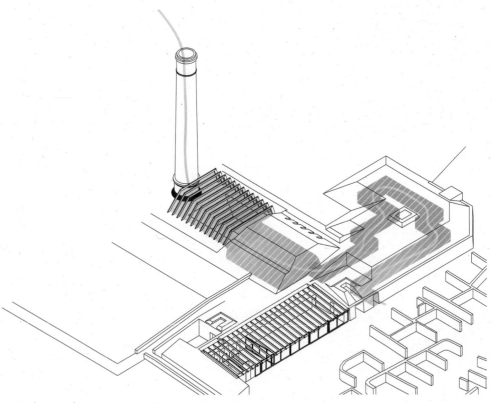

Opposite page top right: Sambuichi Architects, Orizuru Tower, Hiroshima, Japan, 2016. This radical renovation of an existing tower included the addition of an open-air observatory that gives views down on to the adjacent Atomic Bomb Dome and across the city to the coast and to Miyajima Island beyond.

Opposite page bottom left: Sambuichi Architects, The Naoshima Plan, 'The Water', Naoshima Island, Japan, 2019. This project sits in a small village in which numerous old buildings have been reworked to house contemporary art. This former post office was radically reconfigured to serve as a rest stop for visitors.

The river starts in the mountains, with the air and the water flowing down across the rice paddies, past the castle and out into the Seto Inland Sea, which flows all the way to the gate of Itsukushima Shrine. The wind has a particular pattern in Hiroshima, which changes direction every 12 hours. When the sun comes up, the wind blows from the sea, and when the sun goes down, the wind blows from the mountains. The water also has a rhythm; every six hours it comes in and goes out – high tide and low tide – due to the movements of the moon. It's a place where the water and the air are constantly changing throughout the day; it's a town that breathes.

Seventy-five years ago, Hiroshima suffered terribly. After the bombing, they said that plants wouldn't grow there for many years but the plants came back the next year. Study Hiroshima and you'll understand it is because the city is breathing. The sun comes up, the wind blows, the water flows in and out, the city keeps breathing.

On Naoshima, I learnt that we should create something that can relay moving materials. Right now, most people have their own building but they're closed with air conditioning, which sends out more heat into the air. But if we think about the people around us, the town around us, and how our architecture will work 40 or 50 years from now, maybe we will change how we do things.

I wanted to convey this with the Orizuru Tower in Hiroshima, which is a renovation. I thought of the old building as part of the landscape. To feel nature, I designed it so you could walk up to the top and look out to the town, castle, Atomic Bomb Dome and the greenery all around, out to the sea, Miyajima, and that shrine in the distance. You can see the tides flowing through the rivers here too. As with the Naoshima Plan,

the building changes the speed of the air. On the top floor I took off all the walls, and the floor is a hill shape so you can feel the wind and its constant changes.

Maybe Hiroshima is the one of the symbolic places in the world where people can really feel that nature came in and regenerated the town. Hiroshima didn't stop breathing, it was renewed and regenerated. It would be wonderful if people could learn from Hiroshima that the earth can regenerate if people allow it to.

It isn't the only beautiful place of moving materials. Even deserts and other types of climates have moving materials and are beautiful. In different places, people have different clothing and do different things to suit the landscape. Thinking about moving materials makes us think about culture. If we can understand different places and different cultures, I think it can lead to peace. When we talk about architecture, we are making things for people, right? But another important thing is to think of making something for the earth. The earth is also a client that needs to accept the project for it to succeed. I'm focused on continuing to make architecture that works for the earth, as well as for people.

AB: You are pointing to things that in many ways should be obvious, and yet we see your approach as unique. Are you hopeful for our future?

HS: If we work by thinking about moving materials, we can make something that will still be at one with nature hundreds of years from now. That is what I want to do. If we think about changing how materials move, we can harness them and make something beautiful and something that will last. I think that will lead to a beautiful world in the future. That is what I want to do.

Interpreter: Melanie Taylor. *This transcript has been edited for flow and clarity.*

Kari Kytölä,
Paulina Sawczuk
and Satu Huuhka

THINK BEFORE YOU BUILD

Samyn & Partners, EUROPA-Building, Brussels, Belgium, 2016.
The architects collaborated with Buro Happold and Studio Valle
Progettazioni to create a grid system for the facade to incorporate
salvaged window frames sourced from Belgium and neighbouring
countries. This connects the new EU headquarters to the architectural
heritage of Europe, both on a philosophical and a practical level.

Whether we like to think about it or not, construction – the industry architects work for – is one of the most environmentally burdening branches of economic activity on this planet. More than one-third of the materials we extract form the Earth's crust and its flora are used in our built environment,[1] simply because we prefer to build our homes and workplaces out of fresh virgin materials. We hardly hesitate to tear down existing buildings to make way for brand new architecture; consequently, our sector produces tens of million tonnes of waste annually.[2] As members of our industry, architects are accomplices to the deterioration of our planet's liveability, which has led to the global environmental crisis. It's high time we cease to be part of the problem and become a part of the solution.

As an industry, we must leave behind the linear 'cradle-to-grave' thinking altogether. It is due to this distorted ideology that we overexploit our planet for virgin resources while discarding perfectly usable buildings, components and materials that could be returned to use with a hint of creative thinking. Buildings, unlike us humans or other living creatures, do not have a maximum biological life that would denote the disintegration of their fabric and render their demolition inevitable. The challenge for us architects is to let go of our Modernist obsession for virgin materials. We must acknowledge that our new architecture – the way it is currently built – not only amounts to a much larger carbon footprint than the reuse and renovation of existing structures,[3] it also does so at the worst possible time: at the very moment that we are supposed to decrease our emissions as a humankind, to avoid irreversible consequences.[4]

One of the most essential tasks for us is to revise our relationship with the obsolescence of buildings. We must replace the misinformed ideas of linearity with 'cradle-to-cradle' thinking. This concept, popularised by the circular economy pioneers Michael Braungart and William McDonough,[5] recognises that the fundamental mechanisms of our planet follow closed-loop principles, and so should our construction. It is striking to realise that in introducing linear production processes, we have essentially been misusing our only liveable planet. There is no concept of 'waste' in the natural world. Instead, all substances that are produced are absorbed into other biochemical processes. These are the mechanisms that construction, too, should mimic to stand on a sustainable basis.

Architects are in a key position to influence our industry from within. Even if it may feel uncomfortable at first, it is crucial that we expand our thought processes beyond the conventional scope of architecture

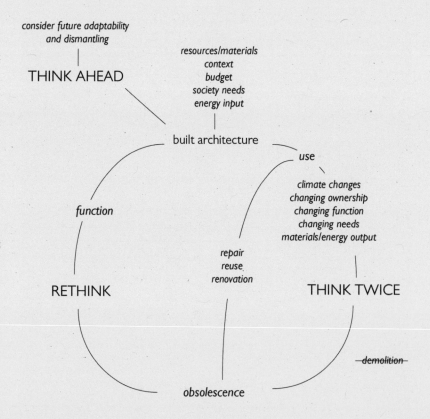

consider future adaptability and dismantling

THINK AHEAD

resources/materials
context
budget
society needs
energy input

built architecture

use

climate changes
changing ownership
changing function
changing needs
materials/energy output

function

repair
reuse
renovation

RETHINK

THINK TWICE

~~demolition~~

obsolescence

The lifecycle of a building project with the points for THINKING embedded. By inserting these three rounds of thinking (THINK TWICE, RETHINK and THINK AHEAD) in the critical points of the design process regarding the building's lifecycle, we can truly restructure the building industry for the better and take steps towards incorporating circular philosophy in building authentically sustainable future.

Flores & Prats Architects, Sala Beckett cultural performing arts centre, Barcelona, Spain, 2014, originally designed by Josep Masdéu as Pau i Justicia workers' cooperative building in 1924. The architects carefully inserted a new function into the former social club, while dignifying the previous programme and giving hints to the history of the building through the material layers in the surfaces.

as the aesthetic-functional design of new spaces. We must learn to innovate and implement new ideas with old buildings and materials so that our artform does not compromise a liveable planet for future generations. We must believe that it is not yet too late to change the course of this crisis.

In this article we argue for three rounds of critical thinking that every architect wishing to be a part of the solution needs to incorporate in their design process: THINK TWICE, RETHINK and THINK AHEAD.

· THINK TWICE questions the need to build something new altogether and calls for a serious consideration of whether an existing structure can be repurposed to meet novel needs.
· RETHINK shifts our view from seeing discarded materials as waste to understanding them as valuable resources that can be salvaged for new projects.
· THINK AHEAD invites us to reflect on the lifecycle of a building and its spaces and materials in an anticipative manner, so that the future needs for flexibility, adaptability and disassembly are considered already at the design stage.

THINK TWICE

THINK TWICE is all about reconsidering existing buildings as creative opportunities for climate-conscious architecture. It is all too often that we conceive only listed heritage buildings worthy of saving. This is a fundamental misunderstanding of the situation. The extensive stocks of existing buildings – millions and millions of pre-existing structures already sprawling across our planet – are in fact our best chance to fight resource depletion and climate change. By conserving, refurbishing, renovating, retrofitting, converting and upgrading them, we can do more with less when it comes to virgin resource use or carbon emissions, as the reuse of the building helps to avoid the immediate emissions from the manufacture of a novel concrete or steel frame.

As architects, we are led to believe, through our Modernist education and glossy-paged mainstream architectural media, that the most important and exciting task we can land is to build brand new and so leave our individual, unique, artistic mark on the face of the planet. Anyone who accepts this idea as the truth

Heatherwick Studio, Zeitz Museum of Contemporary Art Africa (Zeitz MOCAA), Cape Town, South Africa, 2017. The existing grain silo cluster was excavated to create the unique central atrium space of the art museum.

has clearly never had the privilege to truly connect with an old building, to hear its whispers and to experience the unspoken stories and feelings it enunciates.

We can connect to something deeper and more singular than a new structure could ever achieve on its own: a latent untapped potential; the histories and the genius loci of the site and the building itself. Existing buildings can give us a magnificent sense of belonging and ground us to the collective cultural continuum of humankind. Sala Beckett, a former social club in Barcelona renovated into a cultural performing arts centre by Flores & Prats in 2014, exemplifies this by showing the previous layers of materials in the surfaces. This connects the present with the past in a visual way, giving the user hints about the history and previous functions of the building, which each individual will read and interpret in their own way.

An architect that THINKS TWICE embraces the work of previous generations and builds upon it in a dialogue of the old and the new. If we simply open our minds to reusing more structures, ideas for new, creative uses can be sparked for a space as it is. This need not mean that everything must be conserved or that changes cannot be introduced. Thoughtful interventions of addition and reduction can range from minuscule to extensive, depending on the characteristics of the case. For example, floors or walls can be removed, ruins can be used as a base to build on top of them and new structures can be inserted into existing to improve the functionality of the building. The walls can be punctured or excavated to create interesting shapes and spaces, as was done for the Zeitz Museum of Contemporary Art Africa (Zeitz MOCAA) by Heatherwick Studio, where grain silos were excavated to create a unique atrium for the museum. The structure acting as the basis of the Zeitz MOCAA remained vacant for years after containerised shipping became more widespread. This left the building obsolete until an architectural competition launched its adaptive reuse into an art museum. The resulting unique architecture is surely something that would have never seen the light of day had the silos not acted as the basis of the project. This showcases how the alleged 'restrictions' of an existing structure can in fact fuel one's creativity. And what creativity is so fragile anyway that it is extinguished by existing boundaries – that it only flourishes on a clean slate?

Below: Architect NRT (interior design by JKMM Architects), Harald Herlin Learning Centre, originally designed by Alvar Aalto as the university library in 1970, Espoo, Finland, 2016. A former book storage was transformed into a spacious, flexible learning space by demolishing an intermediate floor. Leaving the vestiges of the floor structure visible was a conscious decision by the architects to indicate the previous chapter in the building's lifecycle.

Architecture and the Climate Emergency

For better or worse, the fate of a building lies in our hands: whether a building is maintained, conserved, renovated, or is considered obsolete, gets demolished or deconstructed, or becomes a ruin, depends on our conscious decisions. Now that we know more about the worse carbon performance of new buildings, we should be more committed to making better choices in extending the lives of buildings. Steward Brand[6] has taught us that a building is not a monolithic entity, but one whose different layers can transform to contemporary requirements at differing rates. For the Harald Herlin Learning Centre, the motivation for adaptation consisted of the changed ways of working since 1970, when it was originally designed by Alvar Aalto. The renovation of the building by Architect NRT incorporated the demolition of an intermediate floor so that a book storage could be turned into a flexible learning space. The vestiges of the floor were left visible as signs of the past.

RETHINK

If THINKING TWICE has failed, it is time to RETHINK. Often a building's obsolescence is not determined by the performance of its structures but by the owner deeming it not profitable or useful enough.[7] This makes demolition the most obvious decision, even if it happens at the expense of the environment or local heritage. If we only saw beyond our misinformed notion of 'waste', many of a building's parts and materials could contribute a multitude of values, ranging from the use value to aesthetic and experiential considerations. In addition to their original purposes and visuals, they challenge us to rethink their functional and artistic potentials. Lionel Devlieger, an architect at Rotor, a studio which specialises in reclaiming materials, suggests a conscious process of 'unbuilding', which is the counterpart to the careful and controlled erection of the building. In 'unbuilding', the construction is taken apart carefully and new,

Wang Shu, Amateur Architecture Studio, Ningbo History Museum, Ningbo, China, 2008. A photograph of the exterior facade showcases the intricate collage of the different kinds of tiles, bricks and stones collected from villages that were previously on the site, uplifting the demolition materials to a new, high quality of use, tying together the history of the area in an architectural continuum.

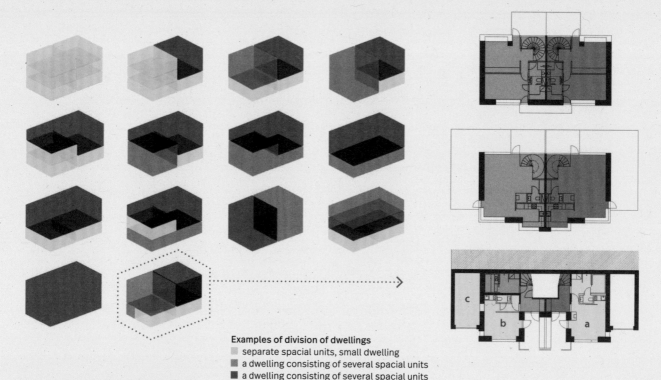

Examples of division of dwellings

- separate spacial units, small dwelling
- a dwelling consisting of several spacial units
- a dwelling consisting of several spacial units

Example for organising the spaces
a. small unit
b. work space
c. extension of workspace into garage

Karin Krokfors Architects, Vanhankaupungin Kellokas housing, Helsinki, Finland, 2011. Ensuring spatial flexibility and adaptability were key principles in the design stages to allow seamless future changes for the residents if – and when – needed, according to their changing living needs.

valuable uses are found for the materials, upcycling them. Upcycling is the practice of incorporating discarded materials into something of a better quality or higher value than it had before. It is the opposite of downcycling – our current practice in which the highly cultivated materials are processed into lesser by-products or filler materials. The arts and crafts of architects and artisans of the past are surely worth more than becoming road fill?

Reclaimed items have accumulated unique history into themselves that should be recognised and celebrated. Cracks, scratches and uneven textures represent the passing of time – which in itself is inherently abstract – in a tangible and visual way and so fortify the user's authentic experience of historicity.[8, 9] The walls of the Ningbo History Museum by Wang Shu (2008), for one, consist of stones, bricks and tiles from the villages that were previously on the site and so commemorate the past. This kind of patina and pastness are impossible to create anew. The idea of throwing away all the environmental and humane contributions to the slow cultivation of such materials seems insensitive and irrational, considering that 'the

time it takes to supply a hundred-year-old building is a hundred years'.[10]

Using new materials is undeniably easier: just click and add ready-made objects from manufacturers' libraries in the CAD programme. Obviously, this is not how it works with reclaimed items. These unique and rare resources do not come off the shelf but must be scavenged. Their dimensions may vary and their availability might be uncertain. Indeed, one of the biggest challenges for reuse is organising the supply and demand. Material map services, where one can buy and sell locally available materials, exist as small-scale as attempts to bridge the gap. In addition to scaling up the availability, storage and distribution, ensuring the quality and recertification into building products remain urgent issues that require rethinking across our whole industry.

It also denotes an excitingly creative challenge for us architects to renew our design thinking. How do we accommodate for the uncertainty and unpredictability of what is available? Instead of sticking to strict definitions for the spaces and structures, are we brave enough to provide ranges that can be flexibly adjusted to match the available materials?[11] This kind of allowance would minimise the waste of materials, so what are the ways to ensure a coherent, harmonious entity that fits the function and the context of the building? The EUROPA building in Brussels, Belgium, by Samyn & Partners provides one answer. The problem of varying dimensions was overcome with a meticulously planned grid system that organises the salvaged window frames into the facade of the EU headquarters.

THINK AHEAD

Every time we THINK TWICE or RETHINK, the environmental impact of a structure is reduced and another layer of history is added. Reusing a building or its component once is a good start, as long as we remember that it will not be the last operation it experiences but one in a chain of many. To be better prepared next time, the logical approach is to THINK AHEAD. The linear society's disregard for buildings' evolving nature is the reason why THINKING TWICE and RETHINKING can sometimes be difficult. THINKING AHEAD helps to predict the upcoming phases and consciously plans for their implementation so that future changes can be introduced more flexibly. This adds to a building's longevity potential.

Here, adaptability, flexibility and multifunctionality are key principles to follow. For example, the housing project Vanhankaupungin Kellokas in Helsinki, Finland, is designed so that residents can expand or reduce the size of their home as needed, enabling them to stay even when life situations change. An important feature in planning for flexibility is the consideration of transformable building services, such as HVAC, so that they too can adapt to different configurations of spaces.

Design for disassembly, then again, plans for the dismantling of the building so that it can be relocated or its parts can be reused elsewhere. A housing project on Lisbjerg Bakke in Aarhus, Denmark, by Vandkunsten Architects exemplifies this. Its hybrid construction is reversible, denoting that it can be disassembled. The parts could even be used for completely different functions, such as kindergartens or commercial buildings.[12]

The art pavilion designed by Adolf Krischanitz is an example of a movable wooden building that

Vandkunsten Architects, Lisbjerg Bakke housing, Aarhus, Denmark, 2018. The housing project was designed with its possible dismantling and relocation in mind, ensuring that the materials and resources will not go to waste prematurely.

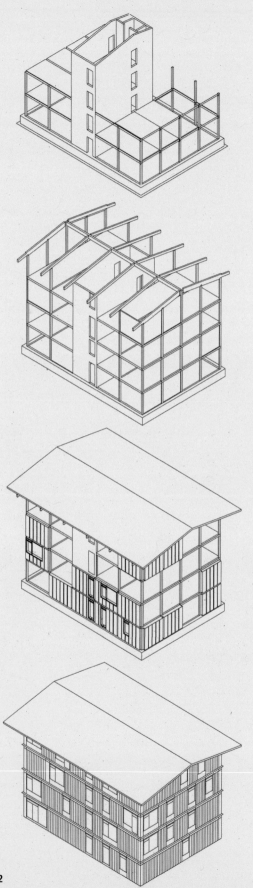

Vandkunsten Architects, Lisbjerg Bakke housing, Aarhus, Denmark, 2018. The reversible construction system, components and materials can be used over and over again. Each house is built on a concrete foundation, the structure consists of solid wood posts, beams of wood or metal and spanning decks, and the facade is made out of precast elements mounted in the skeleton and covered with untreated wood panels.

has already been disassembled and reassembled. The structure is currently in Warsaw but it was first located in Berlin as a temporary art exhibition space.[13] It is a simple white box and its facade is covered with fibre cement panels. The disassembly and transport processes are quick and easy, thanks to the simple, adjustable and lightweight modules.

FROM THINKING TO ACTING

Thinking is the first step to action, but without action all the thinking and theorising in the world will be for nothing. Although an unbuilt, exclusively conceptual project has the smallest carbon footprint, it also has the smallest impact on the fight against the climate crisis. Solely projects that come to life and supplant linear processes with novel circular practices can have a tangible effect on the reality in which we live. Buildings will always be needed as the stages of our everyday life, so ceasing to construct altogether is not a realistic option. The second best option to not building at all is thinking before building.

What if we acknowledged that acting now is not actually an alternative but the only way forward? What if we confessed to ourselves that we do not really have the luxury of procrastinating anymore? It is not a secret that we stand at the edge of a climate catastrophe. Any solutions to secure a habitable planet in the future must be implemented without hesitation. This may very well be the calm before the storm, the last alert before irreversible changes come into force. Soon, there will be no going back to business as usual. This crisis will remodel our industry as we knew it, and being uninformed will no longer be an acceptable excuse.

Just as much as an immediate call for action, this article is an invitation to a discussion about a better future at the edge of emergency. There are no right or wrong answers on the plurality of ways that the concepts introduced in this article (THINK TWICE, RETHINK, THINK AHEAD) can be implemented in architectural practice. We would like to invite each and every one of our readers to come up with practical tools and methods on how to incorporate these ideas in everyday architectural design and construction processes. The time we are living in is one of unprecedented challenges, and none of this will be easy. It is essential that we share our success stories as well as our hardships and failures with one another. Only together can we accumulate our collective wit, wisdom, empathy, creativity and sense of beauty to help us overcome. Join the movement!

Adolf Krischanitz, temporary pavilion for the Modern Art Museum of Warsaw, Poland, 2017. The pavilion had already been assembled and disassembled in Berlin, after which it was transported and reassembled in its current location as a temporary exhibition space, waiting for the completion of the museum's new permanent building. Facade artwork by artist Sławomir Pawszak.

1 Eurostat, 'Material Flow Diagram', Eurostat, 2017, https://ec.europa.eu/eurostat/web/circular-economy/material-flow-diagram, accessed 26 February 2020.
2 Eurostat, 'Waste Statistics', Eurostat, 2016, https://ec.europa.eu/eurostat/statistics-explained/index.php/Waste_statistics, accessed 26 April 2020.
3 Helsingin Asuntotuotanto, Hiilijalanjälkiselvitys, Karviaistie 12/Saniaistie 3, SWECO, 2019.
4 Heinonen, J., Säynäjoki, A. & Junnila, S., 'A longitudinal study on the carbon emissions of a new residential development', Sustainability, 3, 2011, pp. 1170–89.
5 Braungart, M. & McDonough, W., Cradle to Cradle: Remaking the Way We Make Things, Penguin Random House, New York, 2002.
6 Brand, S., How Buildings Learn: What happens after they're built, Viking Press, 1994.
7 Thomsen, A. & van der Flier, K., 'Understanding Obsolescence: A Conceptual Model for Buildings', Building Research & Information, 39(4), 2011, pp. 352–62.
8 Kalakoski, I., 'Defining requirements for appreciation of patina', in Aesthetics – The Uneasy Dimension in Architecture, eds M. Rönn & A.E.Toft, Trondheim: Nordic Academic Press of Architectural Research, 2016, pp. 27–40.
9 Kozminska, U., 'The Aesthetics of Sustainable Architecture: Reused Materials', in The 6th International Conference of Architecture and Built Environment S.ARCH, 2019, Germany: Get it Published, pp. 420–29.
10 Kaila, P., Talotohtori [The Building Medic] 15th ed, WSOY, Helsinki, 2008.
11 Huuhka, S., 'Tectonic Use of Reclaimed Timber: Design principles for turning scrap into architecture', Architectural Research in Finland, 2(1), 2018, pp. 131–51.
12 Vandkunsten, Lisbjerg (email correspondence 2 June 2020).
13 'Museum by the Vistula Exhibition space designed by Adolf Krischanitz for Temporäre Kunsthalle in Berlin', Museum of Modern Art in Warsaw, 2016, https://artmuseum.pl/en/doc/pawilon-projektu-adolfa-krischanitza, accessed 10 August 2020.

What if we acknowledged that acting now is not actually an alternative but the only way forward?

Movement Building:
Activism in an
Age of Crisis

Tom Bennett

Street interventions created by protesters in Hong Kong using materials harvested from the surrounding urban environment, including bamboo and paving blocks. These obstacles allow pedestrians to pass while serving as a barrier to vehicles.

My early twenties were divided broadly between two pursuits: studying architecture and being an activist. When I was not gluing pieces of cardboard together or waiting for unwieldy SketchUp models to save, I was busy disrupting oil company charm offensives on campus, camping outside coal-fired power stations and having my civil liberties violated by police surveillance teams. For a long time my chosen profession and my political activities appeared to be separate, possibly contradictory things. However, recently these divergent strands have begun to intertwine in ways I had not anticipated. This article is an exploration of the synthesis between these two arenas and seeks to uncover some of the possibilities it could offer us in the shadow of climate and ecological breakdown.

ARCHITECTURAL ACTIVISTS

Over the past two years we have experienced a remarkable societal awakening, coming to the realisation at the eleventh hour that, as Greta Thunberg puts it, 'our house is on fire'. For the first time, mainstream commentators are acknowledging the possibility of full-scale civilisational collapse.[1]

Some would suggest there is little architects can do about such problems. Others treat this as a purely technological issue, seeing no need to grapple with questions of social, economic or political nature. A third group believes that architects do have agency – or at least can have agency – while recognising that this necessitates some kind of re-engagement with wider questions of sociopolitical change. Some may reject the label, but for the sake of argument I will call this group the 'architectural activists'. This article is dedicated to them. So, what is an architect's role in the context of all of this? Or rather, what could it be? What inferences can we draw from the past? And who are the pioneers?

What follows is an exploration of these questions, compiled through a series of conversations with individuals and groups making change in this space.

Jim Monahan, Covent Garden Community Association
Veteran architect-activist Jim Monahan became involved in campaigning while studying at the Architectural Association in the late 1960s. He helped initiate the London-based Covent Garden Community Association (CGCA), widely celebrated as a successful grassroots effort which saved much of that area from redevelopment. Reflecting on this time, Monahan said, 'it certainly annoys me enormously that the people talking about Covent Garden being a great success don't also say how it wasn't a success, such as changes in the social mix'.

Covent Garden Neighbourhood Festival, 30–31 August 1975. The garden was instigated by local ironmonger Fred Collins and built by the local community. Festivals and public events played an important role in community organising.

Inactivity is the most political action you could possibly take.

As with many campaigns of this sort, the positive outcomes would not have necessarily been achieved without one hell of a battle.

Monahan believes that the impact of the CGCA may have had as much to do with the receptiveness of the authorities as the activities of campaigners. This is a sobering thought for today's environmental activists who face extreme hostility from a range of powerful corporate and state actors.

When asked how climate change has been allowed to reach such an acute point of crisis, Monahan cuts straight to the heart of the issue: that 'the debate was never about the fact that you had to change the workings of society; it was proposed as just being a technical problem, which it isn't. It's a fundamental change about how we organise ourselves, and I'm not sure that's even been learnt yet because the powers that be are continuing merrily.'

Monahan traces the root of many of society's current regressive trends to the triumph of the political and economic revolution ushered in by Margaret Thatcher in the UK and Ronald Reagan in the US (hereafter dubbed neoliberalism). He is certainly not alone in placing a great deal of culpability for our environmental predicament with this ideology and its proponents.[2]

Monahan links this turning point to architecture's abandonment of ethical and humanitarian aspirations, noting 'whether intentional or not, there's been a distancing between what you do and its effect on people. Many architects in my view are quite happy to go along with that because they're taught that way, it doesn't tax them and it doesn't make any emotional demands on them.'

The climate crisis is inescapably political, and Monahan cites the lack of public control over land use as an illustration of this. He argues that there is a need for architectural discourse to re-engage with such questions. 'People get very offended and say, "You see politics in everything!" And I say, "Well, you see you're doing nothing as a non-political issue. Inactivity is the most political action you could possibly take."'

Listening to Jim Monahan's vivid description of the activities of the CGCA, I am transported to a different era, unblighted by the economic determinism of our own age. However, this conversation also leaves me convinced that architects do have something of value to offer in this moment. As Monahan puts it: 'Get your hands dirty, be awkward and don't take authority seriously.'

Recetas Urbanas, two public school classrooms, Madrid, 2016. The project was built by the school community and is still awaiting regularisation of its legal status.

Santiago Cirugeda, Recetas Urbanas

One practitioner taking serious responsibility for the political impact of his work is Spanish architect Santiago Cirugeda. Coming to prominence in the wake of the 2008 banking crash, Cirugeda has built his practice around meeting community needs directly by working with citizens in situations where the state or local authorities do not have the capacity or interest to respond.

Cirugeda makes a compelling case for architectural activism, arguing that a deeper engagement with the initiation of a project can create space for real agency: 'Architecture students, and by extension architects, are used to waiting for competitions to show their "personality", but in reality they only solve the design of a "building" that is predesigned (and unfortunately often predetermined). Actually, there is no place to comment about site choice, about budget, size, usage, political momentum, users, building processes, etc.'

While many architects use regulatory frameworks as boundaries to their thinking, Cirugeda seeks to test the limits of these through his projects, affirming his view that 'rethinking rules and regulations is not only a responsibility of architecture, it is a duty for all humans'. Considering illegality as an option has opened many possibilities for Cirugeda that would not have been otherwise available. Often the projects of Recetas Urbanas reside in a kind of legal grey area, exploiting loopholes in existing legal frameworks and regulations, resulting in a type of project status that Cirugeda describes as 'alegal'.

Recetas Urbanas, 'Trenches', two self-build classrooms on a roof, Malaga, 2005. Recetas Urbanas often explores methods that enable non-professional people to be involved in construction processes.

Women on site. Working in a team with men and receiving the same status created a new social dynamic that facilitates a dialogue between genders, as well as mutual respect.

Anna Heringer

Anna Heringer is a pioneer of architecture in a humanitarian development context. Heringer's approach is grounded in a strong belief 'that our buildings and our actions and the processes have a lot of power and the problem is we have the focus so much on the outcome and not on the process'.

In her own design process, Heringer takes a distinctively global perspective to application across all scales: 'Every decision, if we consider: how would it be if it was done 7 billion times? If it was scaled up? I don't think that there is a sustainability approach that is only affordable for a third of the world's population – this high-tech sustainability, I don't believe in that at all.'

This approach has led Heringer to construct beautiful ecological buildings using natural materials, often earth and bamboo. She notes that 'the economic system clearly supports building materials that are industrialised that are based on cheap energy sources, which is of course oil'. Heringer makes a compelling case for moving towards more labour-intensive methods of building, seeing labour as another form of alternative energy and arguing for the social justice benefits of a more distributive approach to construction.

Finally, Heringer makes the case for re-engagement with our intuitions and consciences, arguing that 'we have to learn again to be much more focused towards our essential human needs, which includes being in harmony with nature and being a part of society. We're lacking this sense of bigger things that are worth fighting for … beyond a nice award or a nice publication. And that's what we gain when we do really meaningful projects.'

Torange Khonsari, Public Works

Architect and educator Torange Khonsari, co-founder of interdisciplinary practice Public Works and founder of an MA Cultural Commons course at London Metropolitan University, also advocates for a process-oriented outlook.

Khonsari traces industry inaction on climate change back to the fundamental values of the education system and broader profession, which is completely fixated on construction: 'If you're not building buildings, it's like you don't exist, and it's problematic. We produce more and more architects but we can't all be building buildings in an environment where we have a climate crisis.'

From the outset, Public Works has sought to challenge this monoculture through processes of interdisciplinarity and social engagement: 'A lot of our experimentation came through being embedded in communities, and we had to learn a whole new set of skills. We only do buildings we think are necessary; we don't do them to survive, thanks to work from different disciplines.'

Addressing the topic of activism directly, Khonsari notes that the term can harbour a range of meanings and suggests 'we need to have a much more innovative pluralistic idea of an activist architecture practice. Activism means you make social and political change'.

Eyal Weizman, Forensic Architecture

Eyal Weizman is an architect who has made social and political change throughout his career, beginning as an Israeli activist for Palestinian rights. In 2002 he exposed the complicity of Israeli architects in the occupation of Palestine in an exhibition, which was banned by the Israeli Association of United Architects, triggering a debate in Israel around the political nature of architecture.

Weizman is founder and director of Forensic Architecture, a research agency which uses analytical tools and techniques that are decidedly architectural in character. Instead of using these to deliver buildings, however, Forensic Architecture channels its energies towards exposing injustices, contesting official lies and publishing its findings visually, with meticulous clarity. The agency is home to a dedicated environmental research unit, the Centre for Contemporary Nature, which has investigated issues from fracking to forest fires. This experience has led Weizman to conclude that human rights and environmental justice issues need to be understood in dialogue with one another: 'In a place where the environment is destroyed, human rights are violated. In a place where human rights are violated the environment also tends to suffer.'

In considering our collective failure to address climate change over the past several decades, Weizman offers a lucid and challenging proposal: 'The entire economy and our entire profession as architects is organised along an ideology of developmentalism. When the entire society is organised under this meta-concept, it is hard to change the momentum. The problems that we're facing now won't be resolved by a different type of development, but by thinking of other means and modes by which architecture could intervene.

Moments of crisis usually behove radical transformation. I hope the [COVID-19] crisis is going to help us press the pause button on developmentalism and think about other ways of living on this planet.'

healthy forest ━━━ cleared forest

FIRES FOLLOW THE DRYING OF THE PEAT.

14/06

Fire sources

Fire sources

Fire sources

Fire sources

Sources of fire caused by the drying of peatlands for the Mega Rice Project, which was a systematic clearing and privatisation of forest and peatlands in Indonesia for development by the agro-industry initiated by President Soeharto in 1996.

Plenary discussions at Architects Declare summit, the first gathering of signatories to the declaration, Battersea Arts Centre, UK, 27 November 2019.

Michael Pawlyn, Architects Declare / Construction Declares

Michael Pawlyn is founder of Exploration Architecture and co-founder of Architects Declare under the wider banner of Construction Declares. This worldwide declaration has now spread to 22 countries, gathering over 5,000 signatories in the process. Architects Declare and Construction Declares is a global call to action to address both the climate emergency and biodiversity emergency.

Referencing thinkers such as Janine Benyus,[3] Daniel Wahl[4] and Kate Raworth,[5] Pawlyn posits the need to adopt 'regenerative design'. Whereas sustainability is about mitigating negatives and being '100% less bad', the regenerative approach is about seeing how our interventions could offer a positive ecological benefit. Pawlyn is emphatic that to address the situation we face, we cannot use the same approaches that have been tried for the past few decades: 'When we get to the point where as a society

we are having a net benefit on the environment, that would mark a really significant turning point in civilisation, no exaggerations. But if we try to do that, in the same way we tried to bring about sustainability, it's not going to happen.'

To make the transition from degenerative to regenerative design in the timescales available, Pawlyn believes we need a paradigm shift: item one on Donella Meadow's list of 12 'Leverage Points' set out in an influential 1999 essay of the same title.[6] Pawlyn explains: 'We want to bring about a tipping point. In a way, what we want or what we need is not possible today, or not perceived to be politically or economically realistic. But what we need today, is the work necessary to make it possible tomorrow. The sooner we do that, the better.'

Pawlyn describes Architects Declare as a way for architects to maximise their agency – encouraging others to do the same, to bring about this necessary shift.

Daniel Blackmore, Extinction Rebellion

Extinction Rebellion (XR) was set up in 2018 and came to prominence in April 2019 with a two-week campaign of civil disobedience that brought cities across the world to a standstill. In October 2019, XR again took to the streets. London saw new tactics emerge with the deployment of mobile protest structures, including fleets of modular boxes inspired by Studio Bark's 'U-Build' system. Daniel Blackmore, set designer turned creative actions designer, shared his insights on these emerging spatial protest tactics.

For Blackmore, activism and civil disobedience are necessary pursuits: 'A huge amount of change is necessary and I think we will struggle to get that change, but XR has shifted the Overton window.'[7] Along with student strikes, climate change has entered into the consciousness of a lot more people and the bottom-up awareness is having an impact.

The role of creative installations and physical artwork is crucial in protest movements, serving a number of functions simultaneously. In addition to visually communicating a message, these interventions can be hugely inspiring in their own right and enable protestors to hold public space for longer periods of time.

People have been building barricades for a long time and certainly there is a tradition of subversive public installations within architecture from Haus-Rucker-Co to Ant Farm.[8] However, we have recently witnessed an emergence of innovative approaches and creative blockades as a kind of typology, emblematic of what Naomi Klein refers to as 'Blockadia'. In the streets of Hong Kong protestors have harvested materials to create streetscapes which enable pedestrians to pass while creating obstacles to keep the militarised police at bay. These protestors are exploiting the vulnerabilities and affordances of their urban context in a very effective way to maximise disruption and make their point.

Power to the tower: Studio Bark's Nick Newman (co-editor of this volume) stands atop the XR protest tower in London's Trafalgar Square, October 2019. Modular boxes were crowdfunded and assembled into a range of installations from stages to lookout towers and roadblocks, through mass participatory construction.

Architects Climate Action Network

Architects Climate Action Network (ACAN) formed in 2019 and has quickly grown to number several hundred active members organised into a range of working groups. Joe Giddings, Joe Penn and Lauren Shevills are the three founder-coordinators, who hatched the idea of ACAN while attending XR's occupation of Waterloo Bridge in April 2019.

Speaking of the motivation for starting ACAN, Shevills explains that 'you're taught sustainable design at university and I knew it was a good thing to design with these principles, but I didn't feel any urgency. I didn't want to reflect on a career in 30 years' time and think that I'd done nothing about it.'

ACAN has borrowed heavily from organising techniques developed by the environmental movement, from decentralised organising to consensus decision-making. Penn believes architects could learn much from the activist approach as 'many have given up on trying to do things in a different way. Activists never do that, they just keep hammering at a problem and trying to approach it in different ways until they make an impact.'

ACAN recognises the influence architects can have in their work, while also acknowledging the limitations in doing so. The group is trying to generate a kind of collective agency that transcends project-level decisions, allowing architects to step out of the usual confines of their role to affect change at a systemic level.

Giddings explains that radical honesty is also key because 'everybody becomes aware of the problem and then slips back into the normal ways of doing things and forgets to be honest and real about what the fuck's actually going on. There's so much greenwashing that goes on within architecture. Architects just love to talk the talk.'

It is early days for ACAN, but ultimately the group is seeking to build a movement within the industry, unlocking latent potential and empowering individuals to push collectively for wider systemic transformation.

An ACAN and XR protest outside Ministry of Housing, Communities & Local Government in central London over the inadequacy of the proposed Future Homes Standard. The protest took the form of a tug-of-war to symbolise the tussle between local authorities (many of whom have set ambitious decarbonisation targets) and central government who are attempting to use the Future Homes Standard to strip local councils of the ability to set their own higher energy efficiency standards.

Eight Steps Towards Architectural Activism

'If not us, then who? If not now, then when?

1. Architecture is political – take responsibility

'Realise that if you're going to be an architect, you're going to affect society – accept that and grasp it, rather than saying you're just an agent for other people. Take responsibility.'

Jim Monahan

2. Do not over-identify with the role of 'architect'

'Of course, an architect is also a person, a teacher, a citizen. Positioning yourself as a citizen and professional is essential.'

Santiago Cirugeda

3. Break the mould and collaborate

'Innovate, and make sure you have agency. If you find the right partners and collaborators you could actually break out of a moulded arena of work and address the things you feel strongly about.'

Torange Khonsari

4. Think critically and hold on to your principles

'The mindset in architecture, that starts really with our education, is to be compliant. I think architects need to be more confrontational, even at the risk of losing commissions.'

Eyal Weizman

5. Do things that are inspiring and meaningful

'Do what is inspiring for you, what you feel is important. Rather than what you feel will make you money. Do what inspires you, and that will give you the energy to continue.'

Daniel Blackmore

6. Trust your intuition

'When you're really linked to your intuition then you can create an architecture which embeds these questions: how can we be a part of nature, not hurting nature; and how can we be a good part of society rather than exploit it?'

Anna Heringer

7. Remember that another world is possible

'Don't be an optimist or a pessimist, be a "possibilist".'

Michael Pawlyn

8. Act as if your final crit were next week

'Do it sooner!'

Lauren Shevills

ACT NOW

Architectural activism can take many forms then, but are there also some patterns or common threads that weave these together? The need to reorientate our values system and mindset both in education and in practice is a recurring theme, as is the imperative for greater cooperation and modes of working which transcend market structures (that have in many ways catalysed the present crisis).

Ultimately perhaps, activism is about being in touch with the things that really matter to us, at the deeper levels of our being. It is born of accepting that our actions will have an impact upon the world, of owning that fact and directing our agency in a proactive way. As the maxim goes:

'If not us, then who? If not now, then when?'

1 Attenborough, D., 'The People's Seat', UNFCC, 2018, https://unfccc.int/sites/default/files/resource/The%20People%27s%20Address%202.11.18_FINAL.pdf, accessed 7 June 2020.
2 Klein, N., *On Fire: The Burning Case for a Green New Deal*, Penguin Random House, 2019, p. 246.
3 Benyus, J.M., *Biomimicry: Innovation Inspired by Nature*, Harper Collins, 2002.
4 Wahl, D.C., *Designing Regenerative Cultures*, Triarchy Press, Axminster, 2016.
5 Raworth, K., *Doughnut Economics: Seven Ways to Think Like a 21st-Century Economist*, Penguin Random House, 2017.
6 Meadows, D., 'Leverage Points: Places to Intervene in a System', *The Donella Meadows Project*, 1999, http://donellameadows.org/archives/leverage-points-places-to-intervene-in-a-system/, accessed 7 June 2020.
7 The Overton window is the range of policies or ideas which are politically acceptable to the mainstream population at a given time.
8 Schneider, T. and Till, J., *Spatial Agency: Other Ways of Doing Architecture*, Routledge, Abingdon, 2011.

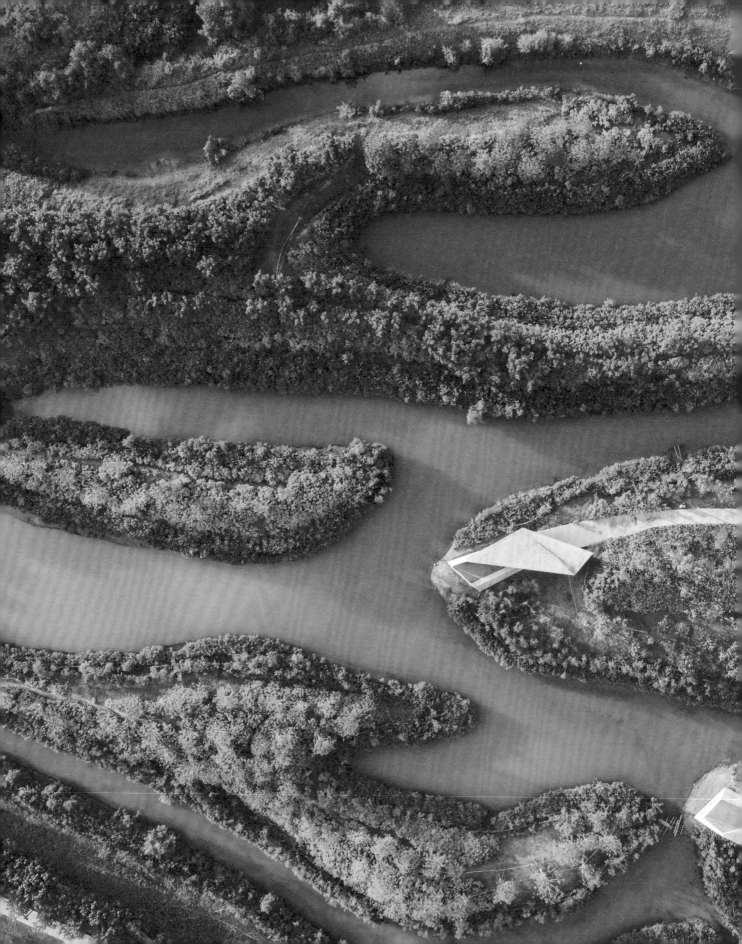

Kongjian Yu

The Sponge City: Planning, Design and Political Design

Turenscape, Sanya Mangrove Park, Sanya, 2016. Ecotone fingers near the river are reserved for wildlife, while those on the inland side are made accessible for recreational uses. Paths and recreation areas are designed to follow the natural contours of the terrain. Pavilions for bird watching and recreation are strategically positioned.

'Sponge city' is a relatively new term loosely defined as using natural landscapes to catch, store and clean water, but the concept has roots that run far back through the history of human adaptation to climate challenges, particularly in the monsoon world.[1] Turenscape, an award-winning landscape architecture and urbanism practice with more than 500 professionals based in Beijing, is constantly developing and implementing nature-based techniques and solutions to address environmental issues across multiple scales, from eco-home design and ecological urbanism to national-level ecological planning.[2,3] It has become a major advocate of the sponge city concept, which has proved to be an effective nature-based adaptive solution to climate change and water-related urban issues.

The Sponge City concept as a nature-based solution to climate change and more

Sponge city: a manifesto

For cultures that evolved with, and survived, the fluctuations of nature over thousands of years, including drought- and flood-adapted monsoon aquaculture, adapting to changing climates is nothing new. However, this kind of ancient wisdom has been buried under the conventions of so-called industrial civilisation.

In the past half-century, little has been done to change the way we build cities. We still rely primarily on inflexible 'grey infrastructures' such as drainage channels, steel pipes and concrete flood walls for building and security, but climate change is challenging the way we live and the technologies we use to build. Grey infrastructure simply lacks resilience.

We need a paradigm shift in planning and designing our cities to adapt to the changing climate. We need to rethink single-minded, industrial technology-based engineering solutions and turn to nature-based and symbiotic solutions. Ultimately, we need to rediscover the ancient art of survival that has been evolving for as long as humans have been on the earth.[4, 5]

It is from this mindset that the concept of sponge cities grew, with an emphasis on using landscape as a form of ecological infrastructure. In practice, the concept looks to provide holistic ecosystem services, including regulating water throughout seasons, cleaning contaminated water through biological processes and nourishing habitats for biodiversity. It is also means adapting to climate change and creating beauty and spiritual nourishment for local communities.

A sponge city requires a fundamental change in thinking about urban infrastructure and the city. It envisions the removal of concrete dams and dikes to be replaced by naturalised waterways, storm water pipes to be replaced by bio-swales and sewage treatment plants to be replaced by constructed wetlands, which use natural and biological processes to provide the same kind of services. Even if this green infrastructure approach does not ultimately sweep away all industrial technology-based grey infrastructure, it offers new options that can complement traditional infrastructure to tackle the climate crisis.

To create a sponge city based on this type of ecological infrastructure, two challenges must be addressed:
1. Finding effective nature-based techniques that can be used at a sufficiently extensive scale to fix the built environment and heal the ravaged planet, while being cost-effective.
2. Breaking through the business-as-usual inertia that favours grey infrastructure.

The quest for scalable techniques

A major challenge in creating ecological infrastructure is developing sharable techniques that can be executed easily and inexpensively at an extensive scale. For inspiration, Turenscape turned to the global – and particularly Chinese – ancient knowledge of water management in farming and settlement-building. For centuries, farmers employed simple cut-and-fill techniques to dramatically transform the surface of the earth and successfully adapt to various types of forbidding environments, using nothing more complex than a hoe. In south-west China's mountainous areas, for example, rice paddy terraces were built across vast territories. As long as 2,000 years ago, Chinese farmers knew that 20% of their cultivated land needed to be set aside and used for ponds to regulate water through the rainy and dry seasons. In China's Pearl River Delta, a pond-and-dike system was developed to transform the marshy land into one of the most productive and populated landscapes in the world. In what is now Mexico, the Aztecs created floating islands to turn otherwise uninhabitable lakes for agriculture and settlement use as early as the twelfth century. Some of these basic, time-tested landscape techniques, such as terracing, ponding, ponding-and-diking and islanding are affordable, scalable methods that can be used today as we encounter floods, droughts and extreme weather caused by climate change.

Breaking through the business-as-usual inertia of grey infrastructure

Beyond the technical aspects of nature-based solutions, it is no less important to build consensus among leaders and citizens about the need to break through the inertia of grey infrastructure, which can require a political campaign of sorts. For more than 20 years, the author has:
· written open letters to key decision-makers, including top national authorities
· published books and articles targeted at mayors throughout China[6]
· given 350 face-to-face presentations to urban decision-makers
· spread the message publicly via channels such as China Central Television.

Typically, the practice is commissioned to design a project

only after spending a fair amount of effort convincing municipal-level decision-makers of the potential of nature-based solutions and ecological aesthetics. In many cases, even after Turenscape has been commissioned, the practice will return to explain the underlying philosophy behind the project in order to build understanding and support among city government officials before they approve the specific design.

Several projects at different scales on China's Hainan Island illustrate how Turenscape has turned sponge city thinking into real, on-the-ground results.

The Sponge City experience on Hainan Island

Under the influence of a monsoon climate and now global climate change, China's Hainan Island, located off the southern coast near Vietnam, frequently suffers severe floods and urban inundation, together with other water-associated problems such as pollution and habitat loss. Those challenges made the island a good demonstration site for China's national Sponge City campaign, launched in 2014 by the central government to test and promote sponge city thinking to address the overwhelming urban flooding issues that confront more than two-thirds of Chinese cities.[7] In 2015, local governments in Hainan, along with the Chinese Ministry of Housing and Urban and Rural Construction, launched an island-wide Sponge City campaign focused on the two most densely populated cities, Haikou with a population of 2.3 million and Sanya with a population of 0.64 million, and we were commissioned to carry out some major projects in these cities.

Beginning with a political campaign and envisioning a sponge city

Taking advantage of the top-down political system, we gave six major presentations on the sponge city concept and ecological restoration that were made mandatory for government officials of all ranks on Hainan Island; altogether, more than 3,000 officials attended. Meanwhile, public mass media was extensively used and more than 50 hours of television time was devoted to re-broadcasting the presentation series, which helped build broad community-level support.

A water-based ecological infrastructure plan was developed for both cities. Each plan integrated areas at high risk of flooding, wetlands, ponds, rice paddies, parks and coastal habitats into a holistic sponge system to retain, clean and recycle water. The plans called for more space for flood accommodation, which necessitated the removal of some illegal buildings in the floodplain. Concrete flood walls that had channelled and reduced the resilience of rivers were replaced with an eco-friendly embankment using earth work and flush vegetation. The design identified areas for ecological restoration and wetland construction along the coastline and waterways to increase flood resilience and, in urban areas, the creation of bio-swales along major roads to adapt to the monsoon climate and alleviate waterlogging. The ecological infrastructure also integrated an interconnected system of pedestrian and bicycle paths. Overall, the process offered a chance to turn the challenges of climate change into opportunities for urban renewal and a transformation of the two cities.

The Meishe River corridor in Haikou City: rebuilding drainage-by-drainage

Given the challenges of executing a master sponge city plan within any reasonable timeframe, it is far more feasible to incrementally carry out projects in individual sub-drainages of the larger watershed. The Meishe River corridor reconstruction was an important demonstration of such a drainage-based project in Haikou City.

Site challenges

The 23-km-long Meishe River is the main river of Haikou city on Hainan's northernmost tip. For decades, piecemeal solutions to the river's problems were attempted, including building walls and locks to control floods and tides, dredging, growing flowers and laying lawns at the riverbank, and channelling polluted tributaries. However, those measures only exacerbated flooding, pollution and other problems. The flood-control walls turned the river into a lifeless concrete channel which most residents turned their backs on and treated as a sewage dump. In 2016, Turenscape was commissioned to reconceive the Meishe as a type of ecological infrastructure to improve flood control and water quality, restore natural habitat and create much-needed public spaces.

Design strategies

A green sponge system was planned by integrating the river with all its tributaries, wetlands and potential green spaces, and to separate storm water from sewage flows. We also designed an interconnected pedestrian and recreational network.

Concrete flood walls and locks were removed. The blocked river was reconnected to the ocean so that tides could once again enter the city. Wetlands and shallow river margins were reconstructed so that mangroves could be restored.

Above: Terracing, ponding, diking-and-ponding and islanding. Many of the basic landscape techniques are scalable techniques for any area encountering climate change.

A major challenge in creating ecological infrastructure is developing sharable techniques that can be executed easily and inexpensively at an extensive scale.

Below: Turenscape, Meishe River corridor, Haikou City, 2016. Grey into green: transforming a concrete-jacketed drainage into a form of ecological infrastructure to adapt to and mitigate climate change, and more.

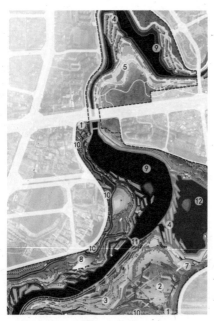

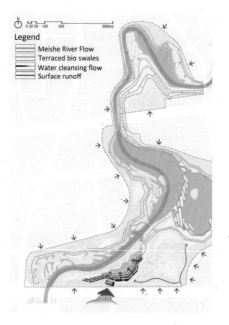

Legend
Meishe River Flow
Terraced bio swales
Water cleansing flow
Surface runoff

Above: Turenscape, Meishe River corridor, Haikou City, 2016. The concrete flood wall was removed and areas opened up for mangrove restoration. Elevated pedestrian paths are integrated with the mangrove.

Below: Turenscape, Meishe River corridor, Haikou City, 2016. Terraced wetlands are densely covered with various plants that remove nutrients from primary treated wastewater, which otherwise would require large amounts of energy to remove through conventional sewage treatment processes.

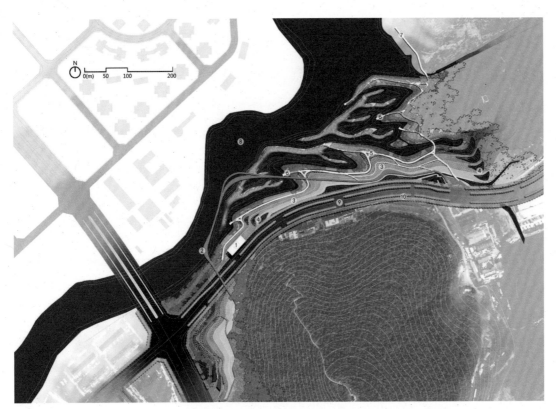

Left: Turenscape, Sanya Mangrove Park, Sanya, 2016. Site plan: the deep form of form following process. Engineered ecotones in the form of interlocking fingers help draw in ocean tides while reducing destructive freshwater flushes and tropical storm surge. The 'fingers' increase water edge length six times, from 700 m to over 4,000 m, dramatically enhancing ecological functions.

1. Main Entrance
2. Sky Walk
3. Terraces
4 Bioswale
5. Resting Place
6. Pavilion
7. Main Path Connected to Urban Greenways
8. Sanya River
9. Urban Artery Road
10. Pedestrian Path

Below: Rendering of the engineered green sponge created by ponding, diking, and islanding

Architecture and the Climate Emergency

Above: Dong'an Wetland Park, Jiyang District, Sanya City, Hainan Island, 2019. The project in progress (2016).

We need a paradigm shift in planning and designing our cities to adapt to the changing climate.

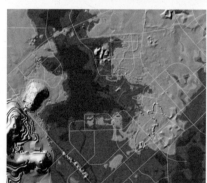

Below: Dong'an Wetland Park, Jiyang District, Sanya City, Hainan Island, 2019. The built landscape of Dong'an Wetland Park after three years.

Dong'an Wetland Park, Jiyang District, Sanya City, Hainan Island, 2019. Post operational evaluation showing the dramatic reduction in waterlogging.

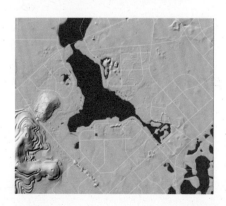

A terraced mosaic of wetlands along the banks of the river was designed as water cleansing facilities that filter urban runoff – and, in some cases, primary treated sewage from local 'urban villages' that are currently unable to access the central sewage treatment system. The wetland can clean 6,000 tons of wastewater effluent daily from grade V to III (i.e. from the poorest surface water quality to non-portable clean water). It is tested regularly to ensure that the water quality is safe and sufficiently clean for public use. The biomass from the wetland is harvested and regularly decomposed into fertilisers for use in the landscaping, creating a circular process.

The project has proven a success. Haikou is now more resilient to monsoon floods, the river water is clean again, mangroves are re-established, fish and birds have returned, and tens of thousands of people have visited the new landscape. Even more significantly, the nature-based solutions showcased in this project are replicable elsewhere.

Sanya Mangrove Park: mangrove restoration to increase flood resilience

To reduce the risk of climate change-driven flooding on the tropical island of Hainan, it is critical to restore mangroves along the waterways and coastal shoreline. One of the key challenges is finding an efficient and cost-effective method to restore mangrove habitat at a broad scale.

Site challenges and objectives

The 10-ha site on the bank of the Sanya River, on the southern tip of Hainan Island, is critical in terms of ecological relationships between the sea and the inland coast, where the daily tides meet with the river's fresh water. High concrete walls enclosed the site and allowed it to become choked with urban debris. The design objectives were to rehabilitate the mangroves and make the site a park. Several challenges had to be addressed, including:

· the mangrove community had to be protected from both storm surge and monsoon-driven floods originating upstream, which can wash young mangroves away
· sensitive mangrove seedlings needed protection from polluted urban runoff
· habitat restoration needed to be balanced with public accessibility.

Design strategies: form follows process

Materials composed of urban construction debris and concrete from the demolition of the flood wall was recycled on site. Cut-and-fill techniques were subsequently used to create a gradient of different riparian habitats, which are for diverse fauna and flora particularly different species of mangroves. An interlocking finger design was used to lead ocean tides into the waterways, while also attenuating the impact of both tropical storm surge and flash floods originating in the urban and upland area upstream, both of which can harm the establishment of mangroves. This also maximised habitat diversity and edge effects, which increased the interface between plants and water and which, in turn, enhanced ecological processes, such as nutrient removal from the water. The water depth varies from 0 m to 1.5 m, creating a dynamic aquatic environment that follows the rise and fall of tides and provides several aquatic species with the daily water-level fluctuation they need for survival. Terraces are staggered along the 9-m-high gradient from city streets to the river and have been augmented with bio-swales to catch and filter urban stormwater runoff. The terraces also provide public recreation spaces.

Result

Just three years after its construction, the mangroves are well-established and fish and birds are abundant. The park has become a showcase of ecological restoration that not only benefits the natural environment but public well-being as well. The approach tested in this project has been implemented in other mangrove restoration projects at a large scale throughout the region.

Dong'an Wetland Park: creating a green sponge in downtown Sanya to reduce urban flooding

Urban inundation is one climate change-driven problem that directly affects people's lives. A tropical storm can easily bring more than 200 mm of precipitation in a single day, which can easily overwhelm conventional drainage systems. Creating a green sponge in the centre of the urban environment is an essential adaptation strategy for increasing resilience to climate change.

Site challenges and design objectives

The heavily polluted 68-ha site lies along the Sanya River corridor, and was filled with non-permitted buildings and illegally dumped urban debris, which caused severe flooding and a noxious odour in the surrounding communities. Meanwhile, public spaces were badly needed.

Design strategies: ponding, diking and islanding

Inspired by the ancient pond-and-dike systems and islanding techniques in the Pearl River Delta, a necklace of ponds and dikes were created along the periphery of the park that catch and filter urban runoff from the surrounding communities using simple cut-and-fill methods. The dikes are connected to form a pedestrian network and are dotted with recreation areas. In the central part of the park, dirt and fill were used to create islands that are planted with banyan trees to create a forested wetland. Both ponding and islanding dramatically increase the water-retention capacity of the park and increase the ecotones between water and land to speed up the removal of nutrients.

Results

The constructed wetland can accommodate 830,000 cubic metres of storm water, dramatically reducing the risk of urban inundation. The property value in the surrounding area has increased from less than US$1,000 per square meter to about US$4,000. It has become a model project for the national Sponge City campaign and has been visited by more than 200 mayors seeking new ideas.

Conclusion: Harvesting eco-services from ecological infrastructure –beyond climate change adaptation

Climate change is real, and it is only exacerbating a host of serious problems that the world is already facing, ranging from floods, droughts and air and water pollution to loss of habitat and biodiversity. While the urban elite in developed countries are worried about how their standard of living will be affected by the drastic reduction in greenhouse gas emissions needed to head off the climate crisis, people in other regions are struggling for basic survival – as they have for generations.

Globally, over 85% of sewage in urban areas – mainly in developing countries – is untreated and pollutes rivers, lakes and oceans and worsens existing water shortages. While centralised sewage treatment systems are economically infeasible for some isolated settlements, nature-based solutions can play an important role in improving water quality and softening the impact of floods, as well as creating public spaces that fulfil important cultural and social needs. In addition, 3% of energy in developed countries is used for wastewater treatment; that number could be cut by 75% if nature-based water cleansing processes are integrated with traditional primary wastewater treatment. Doing so would be a tremendous contribution to the effort to stop climate change.

In the past three decades, China consumed about half of the world's cement every year, yet still only managed to pave less than 3% of the country's total surface area. In the name of preventing floods, China channelled most of the rivers running through its urban areas – but now, perversely, more than 400 of its cities flood every year. If this model is adopted more widely, how much more cement will it take to pave all the developing countries in the monsoon world? And how many cities will be built of concrete without any resilience?

We need to rethink the way we build our cities. Nature-based solutions are not only affordable but also generate far fewer greenhouse gas emissions. As a result, they are an important way to not only help communities adapt to climate change, but to actually tackle the emissions problem itself.

Humans have adapted to harsh and unpredictable climates for millennia. It is only recently that we have become caught in the trap of the so-called technology of high expense, which also comes at high cost in terms of greenhouse gas emissions. Not only that, but it has ensnared us in a Sisyphean cycle of perpetually trying to fix specific parts of the system while ultimately only worsening the environment as a whole.

The shift from grey infrastructure to green is challenging traditional design practices technically, aesthetically and ethically. It will revolutionise the moral criteria and values that professionals are compelled to follow in practice. It will require design languages and designed forms that are not only climate positive but also aesthetically inspiring. It is already demanding innovative green technologies that are replicable and can be inexpensively implemented at the massive scale needed to halt this truly global threat – as our examples have shown. Turenscape is striving to meet these challenges to create deep forms through designed ecologies that will simultaneously make the built environment climate resilient and reduce the emissions that drive climate change itself.

The threat of climate change gives us an opportunity to rediscover hard-won ancient knowledge and bring it to bear on a challenge the world has never seen before. Even more important, it is helping us not just rediscover but actually strengthen the connection between man and nature.

1 Yu, K. et al, '"Sponge city": theory and practice', *City Planning Review*, 39 (6), 2015, pp. 26–36.
2 Saunders, W. (ed), *Designed Ecologies: The Landscape Architecture of Kongjian Yu*, Birkhäuser Architecture, 2012.
3 Schioppa, C.P., Kongjian Yu. *Turenscape 1998–2018*, Libria, 2019.
4 Yu, K., 'Creating deep forms in urban nature: the peasant's approach to urban design', in *Nature and Cities – The Ecological Imperative in Urban Design and Planning*, Lincoln Institute of Land Policy, eds F.R. Steiner, G.F. Thompson and A. Carbonell, 2016, pp. 95–117.
5 Yu, K., 'Green Infrastructure through the Revival of Ancient Wisdom', *American Academy of Arts and Sciences Bulletin*, Summer 2017, Vol. LXX, No. 4, 2017, pp. 35–9.
6 Yu, K. et al, *Letters to the Leaders of China: Kongjian Yu and the Future of the Chinese City*, Terreform, New York, 2018.
7 Gies, E., 'Sponge Cities: Restoring natural water flows in cities can lessen the impacts of floods and droughts', *Scientific American* (12), 2018, pp. 80–85.

raumlabor, Floating University
Berlin, Germany, 2018. A place
for exchange and interaction.

Mario Kolkwitz and
Elina Luotonen in
conversation with
David Barragán and
Markus Bader

A Discussion with Al Borde and raumlabor

Contesting the Architect's Role
through Radical Participatory Design

Al Borde. Left to right:
Pascual Gangotena,
David Barragán,
Marialuisa Borja and
Esteban Benavides.

raumlabor. Left to right:
Markus Bader, Francesco
Apuzzo, Florian Stirnemann,
Benjamin Foerster-
Baldenius, Christof Mayer,
Frauke Gerstenberg, Axel
Timm, Andrea Hofmann and
Jan Liesegang.

Architectural discussion tends to focus on the physical qualities of a space and an underlying process that is linear, beginning with a design idea that culminates in its construction. As many attempts to mitigate architecture's impact on the changing climate have failed, it becomes more important to develop alternative approaches to sustainability. The works of the architectural studios raumlabor and Al Borde show that despite two very different contexts, they are connected through a high standard in social and ecological achievements. What makes them so different is that the latter is not achieved through any environmental agenda nor through regulatory pressure but rather as a product of a high local understanding. For this article, David Barragán (of Al Borde) and Markus Bader (of raumlabor) were interviewed and gave exciting insights into their ideals, professional work and why they make things so differently.

In 2007, four Ecuadorian architects founded Al Borde under the credo to 'do things with less'. Their portfolio includes public commissions, temporary actions, private residential buildings and a university campus extension. Yet, projects such as Comedor de Guadurnal (Guadurnal's lunchroom), and Esperanza Dos (Hope Two) showcase their ability to turn seemingly little into aesthetically, socially and politically empowering projects. Both examples are public buildings that – due to their incredibly low

budgets – could only be realised through community engagement and the use of reclaimed materials and local resources. This practise is applied throughout their projects and, as the footprint of transportation and manufacturing is minimised, environmental sustainability is achieved almost as a side product of resourcefulness. Committed to its local reality, the group understands the importance of community engagement in order to achieve architecture that strengthens the autonomy of its users. Al Borde's hands-on work and the clever use of materials and resources available on site vitalises local knowledge to create a powerful, vernacular architectural language.

Sharing a lot of these values, raumlabor is a collective of nine trained architects where architecture, art, city planning and urban intervention overlap. Formed in 1999 with the optimism of 1960s and '70s utopian fantasies of post-reunion Berlin, the group understands cities as complex processes in which it aims to discover and use what it finds on site through research-based design. raumlabor's attraction to difficult urban circumstances often results in experimental and dynamic planning, which acts as an initiator to stimulate urban participation and usage. An essential part of the practice's work is transdisciplinary collaboration that includes local experts – i.e. residents – in its dialogue. For raumlabor, sustainability is an inbuilt conviction, rooting back to the green movement in Germany in

Al Borde + Taller General, Comedor de Guadurnal, Guadurnal, Ecuador, 2018. The architecture blends into the environment and continues the local building tradition.

the late 1970s and is intuitively applied in its projects through reuse and recycling as the team seeks to work with materials that tell a story. Over the past 20 years, the group's repertoire has accumulated to an impressive collection of several urban art installations, public buildings including saunas, spaces for leisure and work, living, numerous urban strategies and many more projects that can hardly be categorised into any of these.

Alternative methods and self-assessment

Discussing what it means to be an architect, Barragán and Bader immediately mention their teams and refuse the personal limelight. Naturally, there are different interests and expertise among the teams, yet their architectural language and way they create aligns and strengthens their work.

It is an interesting and inviting set-up, one that differs from the image of architects as the lone master builder and spatial génie. Architects are often portrayed in an antagonistic way, aiming to establish their own vision and style in the sea of professionals. Barragán emphasises that Al Borde is not merely a team of colleagues in an architectural practice, but friends carrying out a lifestyle. They acknowledge the importance of leisure as part of the creative process and have adopted a four-day-working week that has led to higher productivity.

Neither practice signs up to a conscious agenda that roots for civil activism, sustainability or a revolution in the profession, but aims to solve the problem at hand and invests themselves fully when it comes to their projects. Barragán explains: 'we just want to give our most to find the best solution every time. It would be quite egoistic trying to follow your own [agenda] as it is not easy for the clients to afford a project and they have high expectations of us.'

In the same manner, Bader replies how, instead of signing a manifesto, the people associating themselves with raumlabor share an inbuilt vocation, doing their bit to make the city a better place of Zusammenleben (living together or cohabitation).

The open-minded approaches and empirical practices applied by the teams contrast with the classic role of the grand architect on a mission. Bader smiles and says: 'What was conveyed during our studies by the university was the old modernistic manner and the self-evident image of a heroic architect, who through his genius and design stands above it all and is able to react and make proposals to complex situations. We were keen to doubt that imagery.' Barragán taps into the same thought: 'We're not helping people; we are working and growing together with them. If I see myself as a help or as an advisor, I place myself above the others.'

Another notable feature of both practices is their understanding and management of the 'human factor'. The projects often show a handprint of the local community, which demands certain spontaneity

and altruism in letting situations unfold. Clinging on to control and project blueprints would make this unattainable. Barragán laughs at the idea of holding the reins tight and explains that 'everyone is excited and happy to contribute ideas and participate in the project. It sometimes seems a big mess but gradually we've understood that even after the people have brought their share to the project and we've learned about the local building techniques, there is still a big gap for us to fill with our experience and knowledge.' Al Borde acknowledges and appreciates imperfections as part of the process, and seeming flaws become part of the design. Naturally, working with the community means the construction phase demands more time and the client needs to be involved and invested in the project. Nevertheless, one can see how the social and cultural values of a building could – as emotional attachment from local residents – add to its sustainable character and ensure it is maintained with care and knowledge.

Instead of consumption and profit, the focus of many projects lies in community activation and creative production. As Bader points out: 'It might be

Above: aumlabor, Haus der Statistik, Berlin, Germany, ongoing. The architects are creating the forum for an urban dialogue.

Left: Al Borde, Esperanza Dos, Manabí, Ecuador, 2011. The architects work in close collaboration with local communities.

Below: raumlabor, Fountain House, Montreal, Canada, 2014. An oasis in the midst of an urban concrete environment.

the time to re-evaluate what professionals and society view as an architectural success. Could it not involve the space creating process and what was achieved through it?' The approach questions whether architects should stretch themselves to use more alternative methods to solve urban issues. It seems that creating more built matter is often the architect's answer. However, linear and classical architectural strategies will not deliver up-to-date solutions for contemporary complex problems. Where do we stand on this as spatial professionals?

The dilemma of whether architects should be involved with social and political issues is ongoing. Nevertheless, it is fair to assert that it is easier to ignore than accept that space influences more than just the physical properties of a place, either in an urban or a rural context. Historical, political and social narratives and connotations are more diverse and should be treated with higher interest and consideration. By rethinking the architect's role, it may become possible to understand the effects and limitations of design, and discover new ways to tackle the issues of this century. The climate crisis, together with increasing population and densifying urban areas, prompt architects to consider social and environment sustainability in order to find ways to embed both in their projects. In adding and combining expert knowledge, perhaps the concept of well-used space could be reassessed altogether.

The use of temporary structures for example, and experimental interventions push the limits of architecture and can create unexpected results. Bader highlights how temporary interventions can help to raise awareness and give us hints of changes in people's values and behaviour: 'I'd like to defend against the argument that says longevity equals sustainability. It shouldn't ban us from experimenting and taking well-planned steps towards something new before investing in long-term projects.' Bader criticises the contradictory actions of the building sector where sustainability gets exploited to justify monetary industrial interests projected in building regulations. As an example, buildings in Germany are required to be highly insulated in order to be more energy efficient. However, the material for the insulation itself is not defined and could be provided by a company with low environmental standards and means of production. Taking responsibility in creating something that does not necessarily follow the rulebook, to question it and find alternative ways to deliver, is where architects can advance.

For both teams, working in a context means to enhance emancipation. This allows users to contribute to their projects and to shape them in a personal way.

raumlabor, the city as a sphere for action, Darmstadt, Germany, 2014.

Architecture and the Climate Emergency

Building with local ingredients and sustainability

One of the specialties of Al Borde's and raumlabor's approach is their understanding of working in a holistic context. Even though it is familiar in the architect's vocabulary and the meaning of the genius loci (spirit of a place) gets taught to all students of the profession, the term's straightforwardness leaves space for interpretation and often results in oversimplification.

The motivations behind the two practice's ways of working are as different as the contexts themselves. Al Borde's approach of working closely with the local community, materials, resources and techniques derived from a pragmatism that was born in a frame of very limited means. Barragán expresses an agnostic stance towards the term 'sustainability' and emphasises how Al Borde practises architecture in a way that is tailored for the group and its South American setting. Environmental consciousness and strategies are not being pushed by the government and high import taxation allows little to no room for implementing costly climate technology to the building projects. The results are more location-specific and hence more efficient. It was a responsibility to meet client expectations with low budgets and limited time frames that drove the practice into working locally. By investing less in imported materials, Al Borde discovered that it could support local producers and have a larger budget available for the workforce. The shift in the financial relation between material and labour allowed it to see the impact of its investment on the community, which creates an invaluable sense of connection. 'Nowadays, money is the rule that measures the world. ... Our search for what is really necessary ... made us use other resources than money. These resources are much more complex to measure and identify, but without them our work would be impossible.'[1]

At the Venice Biennale in 2016, curated by Alejandro Aravena, Al Borde criticised the role of capital in architecture in their installation 'Dark Resources', to underline the important factors that go beyond money and that flourishing cohabitation should not be solely based on constant growth, consumerism and ownership.

Working in a 'radical locality' for raumlabor means to understand the people, to discover the narratives and to critically reflect on them. As a result, the practice's work contributes to these narratives instead of imposing a new identity. raumlabor sees space as a consequence of social interaction and stresses

Al Borde, 'Dark Resources', Venice Biennale, Italy, 2016.
A critical reflection on the role of money in architecture.

the importance of place dynamics by shifting its focus on the dynamics in-between people and between people and a place.

In the Ecuadorian context, working with a community – especially on public buildings – is almost a cultural norm. However, Al Borde does not see it as its role to function as the catalyst for participation but rather the other way around; in its projects, the group tries to build on already existing social interaction and reinforces the understanding of the value of local knowledge. The architect's work becomes more of an incentive for people. For both teams, working in a context means to enhance emancipation. This allows users to contribute to their projects and to shape them in a personal way.

For raumlabor, working with locals means to acquire and activate situated knowledge. Often, the most valuable information can be retrieved from tapping into local experts, people who know a place best: residents, workers, commuters, etc. These informal situations are crucial to understand the context. Spatial expertise is everywhere and often hidden in places where architects can overlook it. It is important to be open to unconventional ways of approaching such knowledge.

About learning and teaching architecture

Learning from one another becomes an essential part of the architect's work when understanding architecture as a social and collaborative process. Al Borde and raumlabor understand the potential of shared knowledge and members of both groups are involved in academic teaching and less formal exchange.

Al Borde currently teaches at UCAL (University of Science and Art) in Lima, Peru. In general, the group regards teaching architecture as an opportunity to share its alternative way of working and values among students. The rough social reality of the city of Lima requires the students to gain a better understanding of the complexity of the environment in which they are working. Barragán criticises architectural schools for often teaching an individualist attitude as opposed to the value of learning from collective work in an architectural firm. His personal experience of working with his professor, shortly after graduation, made him realise the gain from working in a companionable, low-hierarchy environment.

Bader, professor at the University of the Arts in Berlin, Germany, emphasises the importance of connecting urban life with teaching architecture and architectural practice. His desire to work with the forthcoming generation of architects derives from a personal enthusiasm for the future. Perhaps it was the same enthusiasm, contrasted with a critical stance towards established academia, its limiting timeframes and lack of hands-on experience, that led to the founding of the open raumlabor university in 2015. This institution aims to close these gaps by offering workshops, excursions and open discussions which are part of its urban installations, such as the Floating University Berlin project. The space, situated at the former Tempelhof Airport and surrounded by natural ecosystems of reclaimed abandoned infrastructure, creates the perfect stage for an 'offshore campus for cities in transformation'.[2] Here, students and various cultural experts form a transdisciplinary exchange with the goal to discuss the impact of rapidly changing urban environments. The results are learning experiences that are directly embedded in everyday situations in which urban dwellers become students and teachers at the same time.

Discussing its disadvantages, the limitations imposed by universities, on the other hand, can sometimes lead to innovative solutions that are outstanding in how students react to these constraints. The situations that Al Borde and raumlabor evoke

Spatial expertise is everywhere and often hidden in places where architects can overlook it. It is important to be open to unconventional ways of approaching such knowledge.

Al Borde, Casa Culunco, Tumbaco, Ecuador, 2014. High aesthetics achieved with seemingly low effort.

turn teaching architecture into a community engaging dialogue which is too often missing in the academic environment.

Alternative design thinking

Given that 'building construction and operations accounted for the largest share of both global final energy use (36%) and energy-related CO_2 emissions (39%) in 2018',[3] architects need to step up their game. Considering this environmental impact, it is necessary to understand the importance of working holistically and to develop context-specific methodologies that take both – micro and macro scales – into consideration. Ecological sustainability can be achieved through considering local conditions, integrating environmental issues from the start and developing design strategies that build around these topics as opposed to retrofitting costly gadgetry in order to reach energy regulations last minute. What designers can do is to implement smart design that draws inspiration from local conditions and find ways to apply natural ventilation, react to daylight situations, use resources efficiently, be able to collect and use rainwater and support local ecosystems – that is, to have a positive impact both socially and environmentally. Community engagement and working locally can help to carry on long-running traditions and the narratives of a place which are highly relevant factors to distil information and aid urban policy makers in making better informed choices for the future. Architects need to surpass the self-set frames of the common work profile. Al Borde and raumlabor show us that there is potential and alternative ways for developing the architectural profession. That potential must be seized because the risk of severe climatic and sociopolitical consequences are too high.

David Barragán (Al Borde) and Markus Bader (raumlabor) were interviewed by Elina Luotonen and Mario Kolkwitz in April 2020.

1 'Dark Resources – La Biennale die Venezie', *Al Borde*, 2016, https://www.albordearq.com/recursos-oscuros-dark-resources, accessed 17 July 2020.
2 'Floating University Berlin 2018 – an illustrated report', *raumlaborberlin*, 2019, http://raumlabor.net/floating-university-berlin-book/, accessed 12 May 2020.
3 Abergel, T. et al, '2019 global status report for buildings and construction: Towards a zero-emission, efficient and resilient buildings and construction sector', *Global Alliance for Buildings and Construction*, International Energy Agency and the United Nations Environment Programme, 2019.

Transforming Education in a Climate Emergency

have brought us to this point of crisis. Education is no exception: architecture schools must radically redefine their pedagogical structures to meet the climate emergency head on. The shift will not be easy or convenient, but it is necessary.

Architecture students are being failed. Despite spending five years in full-time education, most graduates leave university with neither an adequate understanding of environmental design nor the technical know-how needed to reduce carbon emissions in the built environment.

An ACAN Education group campaign meeting, ACAN, 2020.

The Architects Climate Action Network (ACAN)

Established in the spring of 2019, ACAN has three aims:
1. Decarbonisation.
2. Ecological regeneration.
3. Cultural transformation.

Our volunteer-run network is organised into working groups, each tackling a specific area where we believe the most impact can be made. ACAN Education – the collective author of this article – addresses the barriers and opportunities pertinent to these three aims in schools of architecture.

ACAN Education is a group of many voices: current students, recent graduates, academics, teaching and non-teaching practitioners. We acknowledge that as individuals we are not expert and seek to build on work done by others. Our outward-looking approach helps us to comprehend the scale of the challenge ahead and to visualise opportunities for collective action. We see significant latent potential held by architecture schools and are campaigning to realise this in the shortest possible timeframe.

To understand our profession's current state, we have interviewed some key actors in British architectural education: Ben Derbyshire (former President of the RIBA), Ruth Dalton (Inaugural Professor of Architecture at Lancaster School of Architecture), Scott McAulay (founder of the Anthropocene Architecture School) and Sheffield School of Architecture's (SSoA) Students for Climate Action.

This article captures the key themes, questions and propositions drawn from ACAN Education's early meetings. We start by identifying the state of play – taking stock, so that we can campaign more effectively – followed with analysis of three approaches to the obstacles faced by architecture schools. We demand the universal integration of environmental design, radical activism and increased collaboration, all in an effort to normalise climate literacy and carbon-neutral design.

The state of play

To halt global heating, we have to stop emitting carbon. Fast. Buildings contribute around 40% of the UK's carbon footprint.[1] It stands to reason that architects are implicit in this crisis. As such, architectural education must be equipping students with the tools to reduce carbon emissions linked with the built environment to zero by 2050.[2] Only then can we avoid the worst effects of global heating in the coming decades. In the words of climate activist and founder of the Anthropocene Architecture School, Scott McAulay, 'a non-emphasis on the climate crisis at this point is wilful negligence'.

Although climate change and sustainable design have been taught for many years, few – if any – schools have convincingly tackled the challenges presented by the climate emergency, with ecological breakdown scarcely being mentioned. Universities are failing to acknowledge that the climate will be the defining challenge of their students' careers, as growing numbers of students recognise their own climate-literacy deficiency. Either through lack of knowledge, or wilful negligence, as McAulay suggests, these schools are failing to provide students with an education which is fit for purpose.

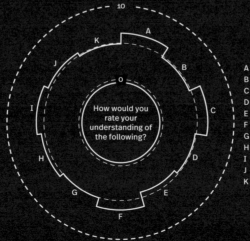

AVERAGE SCORE
5.9 out of 10

How would you rate your understanding of the following?

A   Concept of sustainability
B   Impact of climatic breakdown on the built environment
C   Environmental impact of architecture
D   Concept of ecology
E   Ecology within the built environment
F   Sustainable design
G   Regenerative sustainability
H   Sustainable development
I   Impact of the built environment on human health
J   Passive design strategies
K   Adaptive re-use

Student knowledge gaps in architectural education, drawn using information from Scott McAulay, Anthropocene Architecture School, 2019.

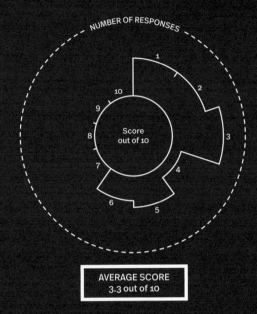

Tutors score students' understanding of sustainable design, drawn using information from Scott McAulay, Anthropocene Architecture School, 2020.

NUMBER OF RESPONSES

Score out of 10

1
2
3
4
5
6
7
8
9
10

AVERAGE SCORE
3.3 out of 10

The manner in which architecture is taught varies considerably from school to school, but broadly speaking all architecture schools have similar informing factors as demonstrated in McAulay's findings. In terms of environmental design, Ruth Dalton told us that there are currently three problematic approaches; the antithesis to the University of Lancaster ethos:

1. Specialist provision (mostly specialist masters courses).
2. 'Bolt-on' (a single module/studio dedicated to the topic, often optional).
3. Ignored.

Too often, environmental design is treated as a marginalised technical issue,[3] but we need to learn how to make responsible design decisions throughout the design process, permeating every aspect of how we design. Only then can we, in the words of Ben Derbyshire, 'deploy our creative talent to deliver the answers society needs and deserves'.

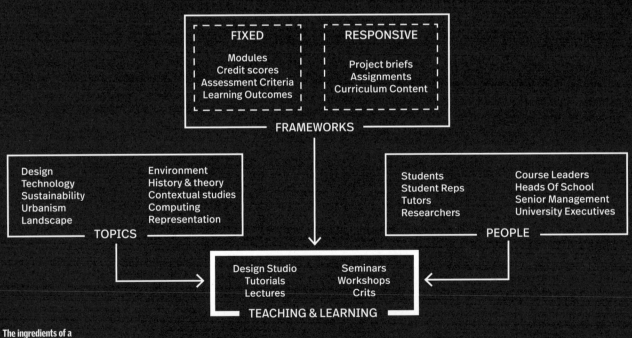

FIXED

Modules
Credit scores
Assessment Criteria
Learning Outcomes

RESPONSIVE

Project briefs
Assignments
Curriculum Content

FRAMEWORKS

Design
Technology
Sustainability
Urbanism
Landscape

Environment
History & theory
Contextual studies
Computing
Representation

TOPICS

Students
Student Reps
Tutors
Researchers

Course Leaders
Heads Of School
Senior Management
University Executives

PEOPLE

Design Studio
Tutorials
Lectures

Seminars
Workshops
Crits

TEACHING & LEARNING

The ingredients of a typical architecture course, ACAN, 2020.

Architecture and the Climate Emergency

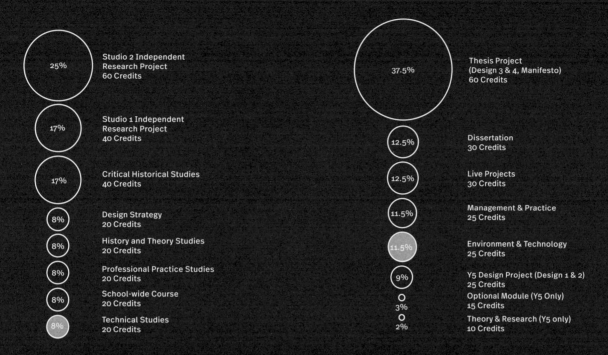

Royal College of Art Architecture MA modules as a percentage of total course credits, with modules relevant to the climate emergency highlighted in green. Information gathered from module handbooks. ACAN, 2020.

University of Sheffield MArch modules as a percentage of total course credits, with modules relevant to the climate emergency highlighted in green. Information gathered from module handbooks. ACAN, 2020.

Royal College of Art

25% — Studio 2 Independent Research Project, 60 Credits
17% — Studio 1 Independent Research Project, 40 Credits
17% — Critical Historical Studies, 40 Credits
8% — Design Strategy, 20 Credits
8% — History and Theory Studies, 20 Credits
8% — Professional Practice Studies, 20 Credits
8% — School-wide Course, 20 Credits
8% — Technical Studies, 20 Credits

University of Sheffield

37.5% — Thesis Project (Design 3 & 4, Manifesto), 60 Credits
12.5% — Dissertation, 30 Credits
12.5% — Live Projects, 30 Credits
11.5% — Management & Practice, 25 Credits
11.5% — Environment & Technology, 25 Credits
9% — Y5 Design Project (Design 1 & 2), 25 Credits
3% — Optional Module (Y5 Only), 15 Credits
2% — Theory & Research (Y5 only), 10 Credits

Deeper knowledge cultivation: universally integrating environmental design

The climate crisis has to become utterly normalised so as to be part of our everyday conversation, all the time. Ruth Dalton

For too long environmental design has been dubbed a 'specialist' sector both in education and in practice, diminishing our capability to collectively confront the climate and ecological emergencies. It is wildly undervalued in assessment criteria, leading to widespread knowledge gaps. This 'side dish' status of environmental design has led to its inertia within architecture.[4]

The core foundation of architectural education is the design studio. The iterative processes it champions endow a deep understanding of design principles,[5] but often exclude environmental issues, reinforcing their marginalisation and restricting what is really necessary: universal integration. Inciting a baseline awareness through integration is critical if the construction industry is to decarbonise. The students we interviewed from an unnamed school in the UK were amazed by how 'little emphasis tutors and students place on sustainability within their design work'. Only by including environmental issues in all architecture education modules, including history and theory, can it be elevated to the level of importance it so urgently requires.

On the synthesis of design and environmental science, Dalton elaborated: 'If we consider that climate change should be integral to everything we teach then there is no need for adding-on "extras", but rather it becomes part of our normal, everyday teaching: you sit with your tutor in studio once or twice a week, discussing your design, and they will naturally prompt you for your environmental strategy; if you are having a review/crit you would expect to be asked questions about your scheme's embodied carbon or type of insulation …; in architectural history and theory, expect to learn about vernacular methods of temperature control. … The climate crisis has to become utterly normalised so as to be part of our everyday conversation, all the time.'

Teaching carbon-neutral design: supporting tutors and students

Students should be taught and assessed on their ability to design carbon-neutral architecture.

With no strict guidelines to competency,[6] the definition of a good architect is becoming increasingly fluid, but one thing that has become definitively concrete (metaphorically speaking – we would prefer CLT [cross-laminated timber]!) is the requirement for carbon-neutral design. Without the tools to supply it, architects are failing their duty to serve the public interest.[7]

Students should be taught and assessed on their ability to design carbon-neutral architecture. This would see most tutors pushed to deepen their own knowledge of sustainable design, in turn supporting students in developing an ethical and holistic approach to design. In order to raise carbon literacy among tutors, McAulay suggests collaboration via 'an Open-Source platform enabling cross-pollination of knowledge and upskilling between education and practice', where the 'collective good [is put] before profit'. Notably, this vision pitches an egalitarian, collaborative relationship, encouraging the flow of knowledge in both directions.

The importance of collaboration

Stop trying to save the world all by yourself. The very idea that we, as atomised individuals, could play a significant part in stabilizing the planet's climate is objectively nuts.
Naomi Klein[8]

As collaboration in our profession increases, so too does its ability to adapt to societal advancements, including climate awareness. Increased knowledge-sharing and teamwork is paramount to this flexibility, challenging the entrenched insular culture of architecture school.

Despite the pre-eminence of collaboration when addressing the climate and ecological emergencies, the model of the design studio typically denies opportunities for meaningful group work. Group projects are often too short on time for students to identify a role, or are ultimately undermined by their assessment using individual grades. Studio culture needs a bold, critical rethink which embraces student collaboration, upholding the proven academic and mental health benefits of working in teams.[9] A handful of schools offer students a choice between group and individual work in studios, as with London Metropolitan University and Diploma Unit 7's award-winning CASS Studio build, and also at AAA in

Denmark and at Tampere University in Finland.[10] A possible solution is to offer a pass/fail grading system as some schools already do (for example, the Architectural Association, the Royal College of Art and Tampere University),[11] encouraging risk-taking and reducing stress. By not offering meaningful group work – both interdisciplinary and within the architecture schools – is to deprive students of vital teamwork skills, without which they will suffer when they arrive at their first day in the office.

Increased interdisciplinary collaboration must also be prioritised within architecture schools. This was broadly on the agenda in the 1980s in schools such as the University of Nottingham and the Bartlett, where built environment disciplines were united under one faculty.[12] Today, broader approaches are also proving effective. At Bucharest's Ion Mincu, architecture students pursue a deep societal understanding through collaboration with peers in sociology,[13] and at the University of Bath students benefit from working alongside engineering students, opening up pragmatic concerns for enquiry.[14] However, this is rare. McAulay strongly agreed with this sentiment when we interviewed him: We need transdisciplinary theses ... purely architectural solutions shall not be the silver bullet. Other disciplines from the built environment and traditional knowledge should be brought into our design studios at every possible opportunity.[15]

Collaboration should not be limited to the university setting. Live projects offer students valuable opportunities to engage with clients, consultants and end users, creating a discourse outside their university. Some schools have introduced live projects that bring together students from different courses, creating scope to meaningfully address complex issues such as the climate and ecological emergencies.[16]

Mandatory live projects at all architecture schools would see students gain a heightened social awareness and skills in teamwork, health and safety and community participation. When interviewed, Dalton, McAulay and Sheffield School of Architecture Students (SSoA) for Climate Action all agreed live projects were beneficial. However, at present a dominant focus on social issues overshadows environmental design. The two should be seen as indistinguishable. McAulay told us that 'students should be involved in "live" projects often to ground them in the practical realities of delivering/evaluating/ retrofitting a building and the up-to-date, sustainable technologies involved'. The design and build project

Most frequent keywords in interviews with architects in emerging practices 2013–18, based on information from Atlas of Emerging Practices, Gianpiero Venturini, 2020

Students should be taught and assessed on their ability to design carbon-neutral architecture.

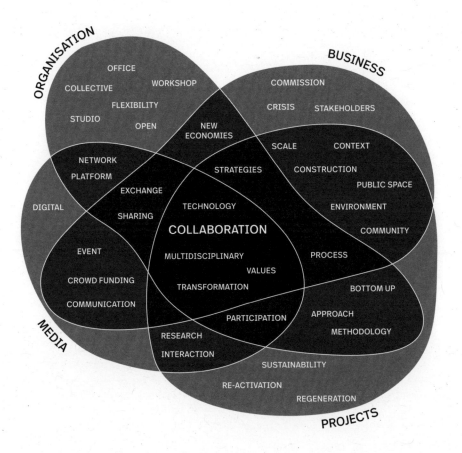

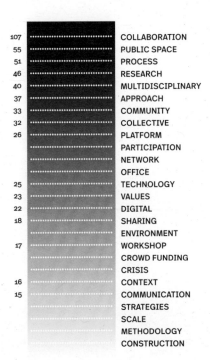

107	COLLABORATION
55	PUBLIC SPACE
51	PROCESS
46	RESEARCH
40	MULTIDISCIPLINARY
37	APPROACH
33	COMMUNITY
32	COLLECTIVE
26	PLATFORM
	PARTICIPATION
	NETWORK
	OFFICE
25	TECHNOLOGY
23	VALUES
22	DIGITAL
18	SHARING
	ENVIRONMENT
17	WORKSHOP
	CROWD FUNDING
	CRISIS
16	CONTEXT
15	COMMUNICATION
	STRATEGIES
	SCALE
	METHODOLOGY
	CONSTRUCTION

Only by including environmental issues in all architecture education modules, including history and theory, can it be elevated to the level of importance it so urgently requires

Typical course framework and influences. ACAN, May 2020.

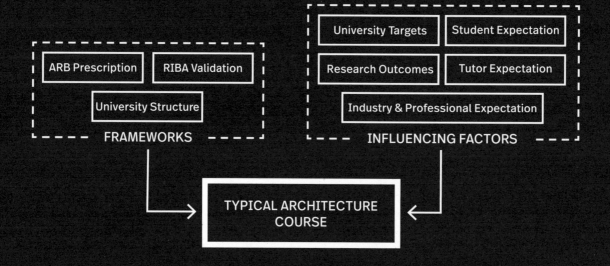

FRAMEWORKS
- ARB Prescription
- RIBA Validation
- University Structure

INFLUENCING FACTORS
- University Targets
- Student Expectation
- Research Outcomes
- Tutor Expectation
- Industry & Professional Expectation

TYPICAL ARCHITECTURE COURSE

at the Centre for Alternative Technology in Wales is a fine example of this, where student designs are constructed using rigorously sustainable building systems,[17] although it does lack the explicit social drive of live projects, such as the one offered at the University of Sheffield.[18]

There is also a dilemma around timescales: longer live projects tend to bring liability and funding issues, whereas short formats often deny students the gratification of seeing their work fulfilled. Another issue, raised by Dalton, is that of live projects taking possible work from local practices. However, these problems seem easily surmountable through collaboration and clear communication. Once these issues are overcome, the live project could be transformed into a cornerstone of ethical knowledge production.

Activism: catalysing change

Activism aimed at disrupting the status quo has always been associated with student life. Ben Derbyshire

Activism has proven successful in forcing change in the wider environmental debate. The school strikes of 2019 and demonstrations organised by Extinction Rebellion catalysed the government declaration of climate emergency on 1 May 2019.[19] ACAN works on the basis that the power of protest should not be underestimated.

Since 2019 we have seen climate activism turn mainstream.[20] Students are now deeply concerned about the environment and are perceptive to the fact that, as fees rise, so does their power to demand change. Consequently, student-led climate groups are forming, for example SSoA Students for Climate Action, Bath Climate Action Group and AAction. Tutors are starting similar groups – such as Birmingham's BSoAD EARTH – Birmingham School of Architecture and Design (Environment, Activism, Response, Transform, Habitat) – but they are focusing their energy on encouraging students, offering themselves as allies when it comes to pushing institutional buttons. This has been exemplified by the formation of SSoA Students for Climate Action, encouraged by MArch co-directors John Sampson and Cith Skelcher. Not only does the group lobby for change, it creates change that is otherwise too slow to materialise, organising lectures and workshops to improve its own climate literacy.

However, while their proactive direct action is laudable, organising climate-based lectures should not be the sole responsibility of frustrated students. The SSoA Students for Climate Action put it succinctly themselves: 'Students are having to fulfil the responsibility of the university for promoting active change in light of the climate emergency … . The university should be pushing sustainable agendas rather than us having to ask for them.' Further activism can inspire universities to re-establish themselves at the forefront of societal development – where they were designed to be.

Effecting change: lobbying at all levels

To ensure success – as defined by the EDUCATE project,[21] ACAN Education aims to effect change from both ends of university hierarchies, engaging in as many influencing factors as possible.

Architecture courses in the UK are prescribed by the Architects Registration Board (ARB) to ensure they meet the professional criteria of the European Union. As the UK leaves the EU and the climate emergency becomes even more urgent, the ARB is coming under increasing pressure to act and, as Derbyshire highlighted, is 'challenged to rise to the occasion with a response that meets the demands of social and environmental well-being'. This year the ARB will review its school prescription criteria and although (based on track record) we expect change to be frustratingly sluggish, once in place these will influence all other institutional demands. ACAN Education will be lobbying the ARB to enforce explicit environmental science requirements throughout architectural education. Using our collective voice we will demand these changes are considered tantamount to the severity of the climate emergency, ensuring schools integrate deep-rooted climate literacy into their curricula.

To achieve more immediate change, ACAN Education has been inviting tutors to integrate its aims into their studio briefs,[22] encouraging greater emphasis on climate literacy in their pedagogy. Despite the barriers of institutional accreditation, there is flexibility in tutors' day-to-day teaching to expand the curriculum. Between setting briefs and delivering lectures, tutors can rapidly change what is taught at a micro level. To support this move, we are designing a framework to deliver guidance throughout the academic year in the form of shared resources, workshops and lectures from within ACAN and via signposting to other industry experts.

Most frequent keywords
by interview respondents.
ACAN, May 2020.

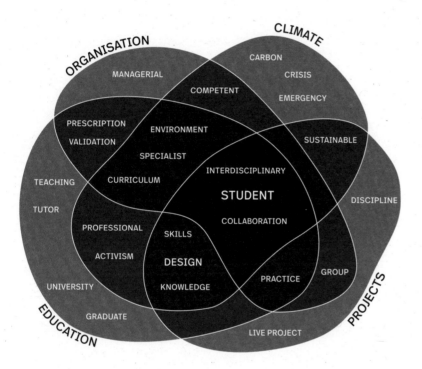

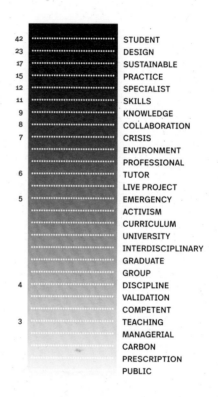

42	STUDENT
23	DESIGN
17	SUSTAINABLE
15	PRACTICE
12	SPECIALIST
11	SKILLS
9	KNOWLEDGE
8	COLLABORATION
7	CRISIS
	ENVIRONMENT
	PROFESSIONAL
6	TUTOR
	LIVE PROJECT
5	EMERGENCY
	ACTIVISM
	CURRICULUM
	UNIVERSITY
	INTERDISCIPLINARY
	GRADUATE
	GROUP
4	DISCIPLINE
	VALIDATION
	COMPETENT
3	TEACHING
	MANAGERIAL
	CARBON
	PRESCRIPTION
	PUBLIC

Hold demonstrations, organise lectures, send letters to tutors and course directors. Take action. We will be there to support you.

Conclusion

A radical redefinition of architectural education is essential. It must unequivocally reflect the urgency of what is now an impending climate catastrophe. By lobbying heads of schools, creating open networks for tutors and encouraging student action we hope to see every facet of education ingrain the climate emergency deep within its psyche. If schools take climate action into their own hands, governing bodies will be forced to take notice.

There is huge, latent potential for improved synergy in the architectural profession but we must act fast to capitalise on it. The construction industry is collectively responsible for such a high percentage of global carbon emissions that the scope for decarbonisation within the sector is monumental, but the reality is that we just are not trying hard enough. The next generation of architects undoubtedly faces a steep uphill struggle, and motivating them to collaborate – to tackle it together – is imperative to overcoming the climate emergency.

It has been difficult to arrive at the realisation that students are being let down by their educators. However, students possess huge sway in the debate, amplified as universities struggle for numbers due to the coronavirus pandemic. They were even the overriding topic of conversation in our interviews. Fundamentally, student fees and education allow universities to exist, and this gives them great power. We implore students reading this article to act on this power: follow the example set by your peers at Architecture Education Declares, Sheffield, the AA, Bath and any other student action groups we may have missed. Demand change. Hold demonstrations, organise lectures, send letters to tutors and course directors. Take action. We will be there to support you.

ACAN Education's focus is action. We firmly believe the scale of the situation demands an activist mentality. In ACAN this takes multiple forms, targeting every level of educational hierarchies. Only when every aspect of educational thinking addresses the climate – and only then – can we begin to prevent an otherwise inevitable global catastrophe.

We welcome anyone that shares our vision for change to join us via our website: https://www.architectscan.org, or scan below. For a full transcript of our interviews please visit the ACAN blog: www.architectscan.org/blog.

ACAN Education Contributors:
Ciaran Malik (Educator)
Ben Pollock (Architect and Educator)
Ben Spry (Part II Assistant)
Ben Yeates (Part II Assistant)
Chris Procter (Architect and Educator)
Finn Harries (Part I)
George Brazier (Part I Assistant)
Hwei Fan Liang (Architect and Educator)
Liv Harrison (Part II)
Negar Tzd (Researcher and Activist)
Poppy Becke (Researcher and Activist)
Rosie Murphy (Part II)
Sarah Broadstock (Architect and Educator)
Interviewees:
Ben Derbyshire
Ruth Dalton
Scott McAulay
SSoA Students for Climate Action:
Claire Wilkinson, Eleanor Derbyshire,
James Harrington, Michael Jenkins, Elin
Keyser, Damien Poblete and Marian Alkali
Thanks to:
Charlie Redman
Tom Moore

1 UKGBC, 'Climate Change – UKGBC – UK Green Building Council', *UKGBC*, 2020, https://www.ukgbc.org/climate-change, accessed 16 May 2020.
2 IPCC, 'Summary for Policymakers of IPCC Special Report on Global Warming of 1.5°C Approved by Governments', *IPPC*, 2018, https://www.ipcc.ch/2018/10/08/summary-for-policymakers-of-ipcc-special-report-on-global-warming-of-1-5c-approved-by-governments/, accessed 16 May 2020.
3 Donovan, E. & Pelsmakers, S., 'Integrating Sustainability through Blended Learning', ina Education, Design and Practice – Understanding Skills in a Complex World, 17–19 June, ed. E. Lester, *Stevens Institute of Technology*, New York, 2019, p. 220.
4 European Commission, 'Environmental Design in University Curricula and Architectural Training in Europe (EDUCATE)', *Intelligent Energy Europe*, https://ec.europa.eu/energy/intelligent/projects/en/projects/educate, accessed 16 May 2020.
5 Donovan, E. & Pelsmakers, S., 'Integrating Sustainability through Blended Learning', in Education, Design and Practice – Understanding Skills in a Complex World, 17–19 June, ed. E. Lester, *Stevens Institute of Technology*, New York, 2019, p. 222.
6 Ing, W., 'ARB Looks to Test Architects' Competence throughout Their Careers', *Architects Journal*, 2020, https://www.architectsjournal.co.uk/news/arb-looks-to-test-architects-competence-throughout-their-careers/10046781.article, accessed 27 May 2020.
7 Bennett, T., 'The Courage of XR Convictions', *RIBAJ*, 2019, https://www.ribaj.com/intelligence/climate-emergency-xr-architectural-arrest-tom-bennett, accessed 27 May 2020.
8 Klein, N., *On Fire*, Penguin, London, 2020, p. 128.
9 Pelsmakers, S. et al, 'Developing Architecture Studio Culture: Peer–Peer Learning', in Education, Design and Practice – Understanding Skills in a Complex World, 17–19 June, ed. E. Lester, *Stevens Institute of Technology*, New York, 2019, p. 264.
10 AJ Building Library, 'CASS Studio Unit 7, The Cass, Huntingdon, 2019', *AJ Building Library*, https://www.ajbuildingslibrary.co.uk/projects/display/id/8376, accessed 6 June 2020.
11 Personal communication with S. Pelsmakers, May 2020.
12 Hall, P., 'Richard Llewelyn Davies, 1912–1981: A Lost Vision for the Bartlett', in *Forty Ways to Think about Architecture: Architectural History and Theory Today*, eds. I. Borden, M. Fraser & B. Penner, Wiley, Chichester, 2014, pp. 214-19.
13 Studio Basar, *City School 1*, 2015–16, http://www.studiobasar.ro/?p=7136&lang=en, accessed 1 June 2020.
14 University of Bath, 'Department of Architecture & Civil Engineering', *University of Bath*, 2020, https://www.bath.ac.uk/departments/department-of-architecture-civil-engineering/, accessed 27 May 2020.
15 Lawrence, R.J., 'Deciphering Interdisciplinary and Transdisciplinary Contributions', *Transdisciplinary Journal of Engineering & Science*, Vol. 1, issue 1, 2010, p. 125.
16 Including Central St Martins, Oxford Brookes, the Royal College of Art, the University of East London and the University of Sheffield.
17 Centre for Alternative Technology, 'Masters in Sustainable Architecture – ARB Part II', *Centre for Alternative Technology*, 2020, https://www.cat.org.uk/courses-and-training/graduate-school/courses/march-sustainable-architecture/, accessed 18 May 2020.
18 The University of Sheffield School of Architecture, 'Live Projects', *Live Projects*, 2020, http://www.liveprojects.org/, accessed 31 May 2020.
19 Turney, C., 'UK Becomes First Country to Declare a "Climate Emergency"', *The Conversation*, 2019, https://theconversation.com/uk-becomes-first-country-to-declare-a-climate-emergency-116428, accessed 27 May 2020.
20 Klein, N., *On Fire*, Penguin, London, 2020, pp. 1–25.
21 European Commission, 'Environmental Design in University Curricula and Architectural Training in Europe (EDUCATE)', *Intelligent Energy Europe*, https://ec.europa.eu/energy/intelligent/projects/en/projects/educate, accessed 16 May 2020.
22 Visit https://www.architectscan.org/home to see ACAN's aims in full.

Elizabeth Donovan, Urszula Kozminska, Nacho Ruiz Allen and Thomas R. Hilberth

Architectural Learning
for a Sustainable Future

Marleen Stokkeby, Resist
and Resign, Løgstør,
Denmark, 2018. The
passage of time and decay
in a rose oil production
and water baths.

The climate is changing. More powerful storms, more heat waves, more precipitation, rising sea level and average temperatures are predicted globally. The future scenario graduating students will face as they enter the workforce is unpredictable, and educating for this is a common challenge. Business as usual is no longer an option and continuing to be 'less bad' is destroying our planet. Students are now demanding change as they see the ability to meet their future needs being compromised. Fostering and emboldening the energy and dedication students have towards these issues is crucial to successfully make changes in educating for the climate emergency. However, this is not a simple task. The architect's role is crucial and educators must encourage students to question their future position and responsibilities in shaping new solutions to replace an inadequate status quo.

Rather than providing the students with predefined conclusions on how to solve specific problems, students must be enabled to gain an understanding of the tasks' inherent complexities, learning to navigate within a dynamic catalogue of relevant questions rather than being provided with fixed answers and rules. The goal is to empower future architects through the knowledge and understanding that is required to develop a critical mind. This allows them to find their own individual but contextually appropriate response to an architectural assignment. Design tasks should involve holistic sustainable thinking from the beginning and assignments should acknowledge our environmental challenges as a point of departure while still aiming to create beautiful spaces and buildings which respect our finite resources. Only aesthetic outcomes are truly sustainable and will endure under public scrutiny.

AAA is one of two beaux-arts based architecture schools in Denmark, with a long tradition for developing sustainable architecture. The teaching programme, Emerging Sustainable Architecture, is grounded in contextual design, encouraging plural and holistic approaches to sustainable architecture. It is supported by emerging pedagogies which address global and local challenges in society, encouraging a thorough understanding of context as a necessary precondition to conceive and construct spaces for the needs and well-being of people and the environment. Contextual influences in an assignment are found in politics, history, culture, ethics, climate/change, pollution, ecology, (scarce) resources, economy and technology. They are approached by involving trans-disciplinary tools from fields such as anthropology, sociology and psychology to foster new qualities and imagination within the student's architectural project. These contextual influences enrich and inspire rather than inhibit the architectural design process to create the foundation for a resilient and healthy environment in the shifting Anthropocene.

Students engage with concepts such as 'think global, act local' to understand further the far-reaching consequences local decisions can have on the global society and vice versa. They learn how to navigate both the complex whole and the micro details of site-specific necessities. Subsequently, the curriculum usually encompasses both sustainable projects with an international background as well as tasks anchored in the very local Danish or Nordic conditions.

To strengthen creative thinking, individual design assignments always contain and expect strong narratives and encourage the students to influence the brief and to develop their own architectural position and programme. Topics may include aspects of environmental challenges, climate change, migration patterns and social issues, as well as possible future developments and more speculative scenarios while embracing the qualities of time and poetics where aesthetics always plays an essential role in the overall outcome.

One masters studio and two bachelor's units are described below, highlighting the different approaches to educating students for the climate emergency. They also illustrate how sustainable architectural thinking and design can be integrated to confront a diverse and complex world in desperate need of change.

Below and opposite page: Wanda Van Roey, The Hidden Patio, Hershey, Cuba, 2019. A hemp farm, workshop and community area in Hershey.

Studio 3:
Shifting territories for an (un)stable environment

The world has shifted. Several decades ago it could be described as a long-lasting and limitless entity; however, this no longer holds true. Today we are faced with a quality that overtakes the previous ones: impermanence. Architecture and its discourse thrived in a world of abundance and optimism but we are now confronted with the environmental, health and climatic impacts of our culture in a finite world. Hence, architecture and its discourse are shifting too.

How will we live and work now and in the future within this shifting world? What about the spaces we inhabit and the architecture we conceive? Has our physical context also acquired a shifting condition? Infrastructures, constructions, landscapes and even what we mistakenly denominate as nature are undergoing processes of perpetual transformation at all scales. The ever-present factor of time in architecture gains significance and creates a new setting for addressing climate change adaptation, and these are considerations which frame the pedagogies within Studio 3.

At Studio 3, the aim is to critically investigate the production of architecture under unstable territorial and environmental conditions, both now and as imagined – shifted – in the future. There is an open and experimental approach towards sustainable architecture where the idea of time is at the core of each investigation. The overall goal is that the students formulate, test and develop their own architectural agenda, responding to site-specific programmatic, environmental and material contexts over time. It is about designing architectural scenarios, not objects.

Studio 3 has explored the power of architectural imagination in overlapping, unstable and even disappearing landscapes due to natural threats and/or socio-economic disparities. The students developed their work in small settlements facing similar processes of depopulation, loss of identity and climate change.

For example, in Løgstør, situated in an inner fjord in Denmark, the students were confronted with the speculated sea-level rise and the increasing impact of seasonal storms. This challenge was addressed functionally and poetically. Several projects expressively broke the linear evolution of time by merging present and future aspects into one single narrative. This is exemplified by the case of Marleen Stokkeby's rose oil production and water baths, which questions two opposites present in the town: the passage of time and the aim of freezing the moment. The proposal radically explores decay by combining materials with different robustness. Shaped as an elevated structure that bridges the ridge and the old town, the project is expected to experience changes within a couple of months, in the chalk walls and over several decades in the structural steel elements (see images pp 76-77). The curated disintegration of the entire design suggests its future use as a pier and, at the same time, questions this possibility due to its material obsolescence.

Subsequently, a visit to Hershey (Camilo Cienfuegos), Cuba, aimed to critically reflect on how to address societal and environmental challenges in unfamiliar territories. Most of the students focused on the economic revitalisation of the town by analysing its resources and turning them into productive goods for the local community. For instance, Wanda Van Roey created a hemp textile production facility using vegetation as the

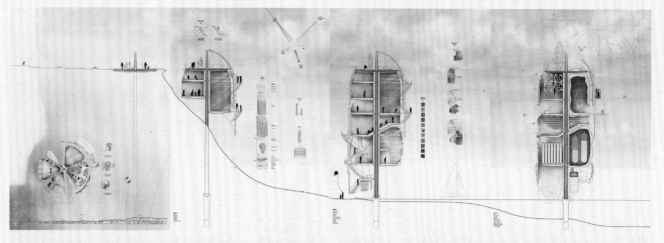

Hugo Shackleton, Landmark, Lønstrup, Denmark, 2019. Addressing a shifting landscape of the Danish West coast in a future scenario.

main design element that creates a natural wind flow for cooling down, protects from excessive heating and enriches biodiversity. The centre, which includes social areas, is hidden from the busy streets by plants until they are harvested in the rainy season. The constructions are of rammed earth and bamboo, and are built and expanded by the community itself.

Back in Denmark, the students designed spaces for a small community of architects in Lønstrup, a place on the west coast where the sea takes away 3 m of land per year while dunes move 30 m inland via sand-drift. These extreme environmental conditions inspired experimental proposals addressing different lifespans and evolution patterns of the designed buildings. Alexander Hugo Shackleton has proposed a vertical column which is initially buried in the ground and will slowly protrude from the cliff as erosion takes place. While the column becomes gradually exposed, structural slabs can be easily attached and transformed into liveable spaces, in close intimacy with the strata of the vertical ground. In the last stage, the building's 'turbine-like' steel structure has the potential to become a piece of offshore infrastructure and a marker of passing time.

All these projects show the power of scenario thinking as a driver for architectural imagination in a context of the climate emergency, reminding us that time is a core aspect when constructing, experiencing and inhabiting architecture. It is also time to introduce its influence to the design phase of architecture.

Architecture and the Climate Emergency

Unit 2/3F:
Habitation+ – the story of an urban settlement in Cuba

The complexity of the climate emergency is a crucial and challenging topic for undergraduate students. Unit 2/3F approaches these issues through choosing topics and locations for semester projects which allow the students to address various societal and environmental challenges from their own interest. Bachelor students explored social interactions within complex ecosystems of constantly appropriated and sustained Cuban cities. Hershey and Vedado in Havana served as two locations for inspiration to discuss urban density, city dynamics, climate change, the reuse of existing buildings and materials, as well as individualisation of housing typologies.

In Cuba, the housing shortage is provoked by failed policies, low housing production and an uncertain future. The inhabitants of Havana overcome their housing problems by reinventing the city from the outside, in. These often-improvised appropriations of space tell a lot about human living conditions and the needs of its users.

Students examined the necessities of local architecture, do-it-yourself appropriations and diverse city transformations. They negotiated between the immediate and provisional, the unfinished and complete, the permanent and progressive. They explored private and public spaces as well as formal and informal developments.

Investigations in Cuba focused on the diverse ways of living in the city, on different modes of participation in the public domain and on specific social orders, understanding certain spatial choreographies which dictate how people can co-exist through elements and codes. More subtle choreographies of social spaces were also discovered, such as the unwritten rules of behaviour and specific urban identities which invite society to participate or observe. These explorations showed how locals are influenced by the city which faces climate change and how architecture is affected by their needs, customs and practices. The students learnt from users and their relation to the city through participatory observation, interviews, planned walks and diverse designed and informal interactions with the locals. They translated ordinary local routines – often affected by shifting climatic conditions – into architectural projects to create the space which can address diverse needs of its users and which can contribute to daily human lives.

Students mapped and analysed social interactions, climatic conditions and requirements of local communities in Hershey and Havana to design a building which contained habitation plus a city-forming function. This open brief required the students to self-programme and to develop their own approach to the project and site. The projects focused on the interdependencies between the activity of the community, ways of living, housing typologies and scarcity of available resources. With many students developing programmes which resulted in self-sufficient models of co-living and co-working, based on shared economy principles, sustainable use of land, resources, structures and local skills, the outcome of the semester was vast in concepts and diversity. David Westervik transformed a dock structure situated by the Almendares River into a recycling centre combined with a living space for local waste pickers – a socially stigmatised group of users – which in the new programme not only contributes to the circular flow

David Westervik, Reuse Station, Havana, 2019. Working with local waste to erase social stigma through the use of a modular construction system (left) to create an easy framework for the implementations of recycled materials, such as creating a climate screen (middle) made from glass bottles which can easily be prepared manually (right).

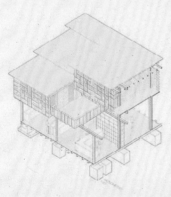

of the materials within the city but also gains social significance. Another example is by Malthe Andreassen, who adapted the same existing building for an inhabitable urban farming complex, which introduces an aquaponics system to use the potential of the river to ensure food security and to create new workplaces for the local community.

Johann Klause extended the structure to create flexible and affordable living units, which can be adapted by their users with the systems produced in the existing workshop. In Hershey, Niclas Heydron transformed an abandoned hotel into an open market with diverse service stalls and repair workshops which used locally available resources and skills, incorporating alternative co-living typologies. In the same town, Mads Lyhne designed the co-living building with permaculture production in a deserted water-cooling tower. Phuong Uyen Nguyen re-established a material lab with a ceramics workshop to produce essential building elements, and Ida Thallaug used the existing concept of CASAS particulars (short-term co-living for tourists and locals) to create a hotel which economically supports the local community.

The architectural explorations in Cuba were diverse, demonstrating that multidisciplinary working methods and a willingness to learn from an unfamiliar context results in architecture which is developed and used by people and which also creates space for human interactions and builds resilient communities in times of a changing climate.

Above: Johann Klause, Robust Architecture in Havana, 2019. Creating diversity through a flexible facade system.

Right: Malthe Andreassen, Inhabitable Gardens, Cuba, 2019. The ecology of living, inhabiting urban food production.

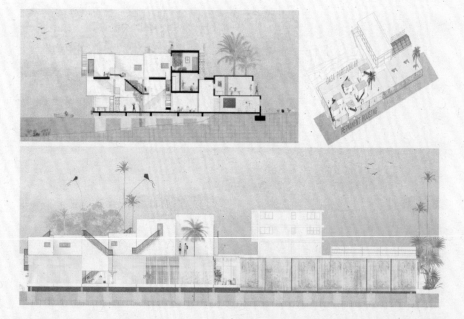

Architecture and the Climate Emergency

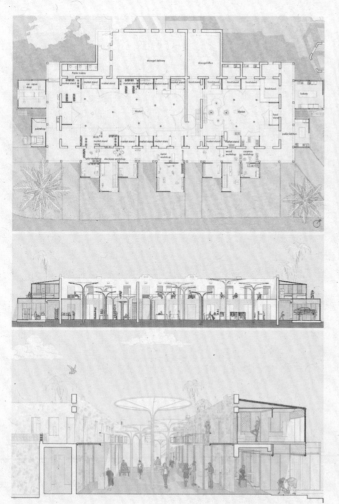

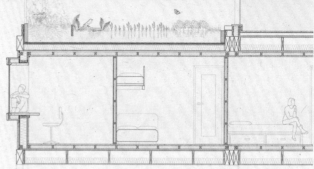

Left: Niclas Heydron, Hershey's Trading Market, Cuba, 2019. Co-living in a shared space for exchange of local skills and resources.

Above: Isak D. Sønderland, The Kapok Tree Community, Vejle, Denmark, 2019. Combining flexibility, adaptability and biodiversity in a future scenario of extreme environmental degradation.

Unit 2/3E:
Unit E – sustainable architecture and resources

Two things are clear – we are running out of resources, and the climate is changing. Students from Unit 2/3E faced the challenge of how to envision a future scenario in which the current crisis is a design driver rather than a hindrance. History shows that the re-use of resources has been a common practice. However, within modern architecture of the twentieth century this practice was abandoned to a building culture relying on an industrialised production of new components – which far too often ends up in landfill sites. To address this issue of material flows and reuse, students were asked to design a strategy for habitation combined with a resilient production on the given complex and challenging site of the old landfill in Vejle, Denmark. The site has a rich and diverse history and is characterised as an industrial zone neighboured by

urban developments as well as nature that connects with the greater city. This chosen site required students to not only reconsider the lifecycles of resources but also how to design in an area threatened by potential sea-level rise and extensive flooding.

Within the open brief, both second and third year students were encouraged to explore sustainable approaches to architecture from whichever perspective they found most inspiring, creating narratives and future scenarios for a more resilient city within the context of a continuously changing climate. An open brief allowed for many different approaches, such as Isak D. Sønderland who used the Kapok tree as a source of inspiration to create a new community set 20 years in the future where people no longer treat human-caused climate change as a theory. In his scenario, the planet's biodiversity has decreased tremendously. The project integrates the complexity of nature within a modular system that can

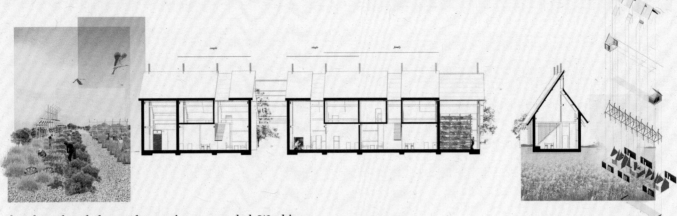

be altered and changed over time as needed. Working with principles of resilience and design for disassembly, the community combines a series of flexible and moveable, 'green-roofed' modules which can respond to the changing climate through a considerable increase of biodiversity.

Similarly, Christian Simon Reese Reinholdt Andersen explored a fictional scenario in which climate change has caused 6 m of sea-level rise, flooding the site. The project, Soapnut Community, questions how society can settle on the water and reduce waste production as well as avoiding further water pollution. Embracing the water, it speculates a future of water-based living and transport. Below the platform is a diversity of activities – houseboats, natural plant-based cleaning systems and transportation – while above, different-sized settlements and buildings form structures around the soap tree houses.

Second-year students Toya Causse and Frida Nordvik worked as a pair to create a community exploring how plants can work to cleanse the soil of the toxic site as well as how food production and processes can bring communities together, focusing on apples as an undervalued resource in Denmark. Their community consisted of public gardens, housing, a juice press and a restaurant. Toya and Frida use the fairy tale, The Nightingale by Hans Christian Andersen, as an architectural tool, noting the area's forgotten potential and bringing back the qualities which were once visible in the site. The project acts over time in different phases, starting with the cleansing of the soil, the establishment of the garden which is maintained by the residents and citizens into the future.

While faced with an immensely complex site and brief, students designed and envisioned new scenarios which pushed the boundaries of how we occupy land, habitation patterns and the use of resources accepting climate change as an inevitable future condition.

Above: Toya Causse and Frida Nordvik, The Juice Press Garden and Community, Denmark, 2019. Using narratives to rediscover potentials of place.

Below and opposite: Christian S.R.R. Andersen, Soapnut Community, Vejle, Denmark, 2019. A future scenario for living with the water in a changing climate

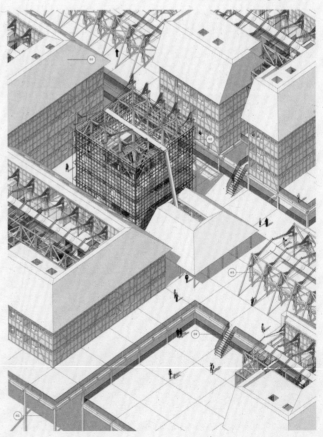

Conclusion

There is a diversity of approaches and pedagogies in how sustainable architecture can be addressed to meet the needs of our changing climate. The future challenges which the architecture profession faces are fundamental to address and are considered design opportunities for both teaching and learning. Examples of different teaching environments and student work illustrate the flexibility and ownership students are given within their studio-based education. Within the framework of challenging sites and contexts, students are encouraged to find their own position, approach and method for how they want to be an architect of the future.

Students, educators and architects must not accept business as usual and instead they must be critical, questioning the status quo and the role of designers. They must fight for a better future. They need to be agile and embrace the complexity and consequences of an uncertain environment. They need to understand the predicament as an opportunity to make change rather than to consider it a hindrance.

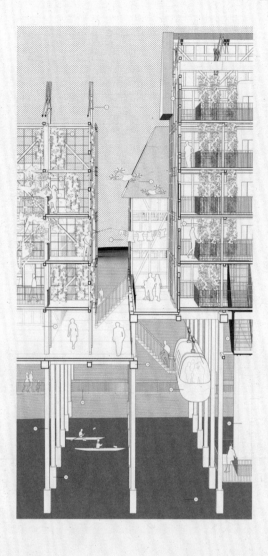

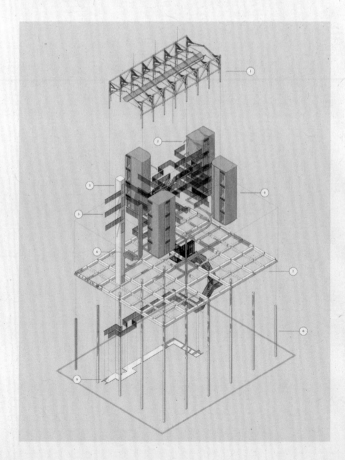

Students, educators and architects must not accept business as usual and instead they must be critical, questioning the status quo and the role of designers.

Acknowledgements
Studio 3 teachers:
Nacho Ruiz Allen, Ula Kozminska, Mads Nygaard, Mads Bay Møller, Tommy Bruun, Stine Schmidt, Martin Ringstrøm, Sofie Pelsmakers
Unit 2/3F teachers: Urszula Kozminska, Thomas R. Hilberth, Eva Rosborg Aagaard, Kim Olesen, Troels Thorbjørnson
Unit 2/3E teachers: Heidi Merrild, Troels Rugbjerg, Elizabeth Donovan

ANTI-CAPITALIST
FEMINISTS

Sanjukta Jitendhar, key image of the project Manifesto. Student project, Ecosystem City Studio, SSoA, 2018/19.

Hope in the Burning World

Kasia Nawratek

Only a crisis – actual or perceived – produces real change. When that crisis occurs, the actions that are taken depend on the ideas that are lying around. That, I believe, is our basic function: to develop alternatives to existing policies, to keep them alive and available until the politically impossible becomes the politically inevitable.[1] Milton Friedman

This quote appears in a new book by Bram Büscher and Robert Fletcher, *The Conservation Revolution: Radical Ideas for Saving Nature Beyond the Anthropocene*,[2] which proposes a new model for nature conservation called the Convivial Conservation based on ideas such as degrowth and Conservation Basic Income. It also appears in Naomi Klein's short film[3] discussing the economic impact of the coronavirus. Klein questioned further, asking: 'But whose ideas? Sensible, fair ones, designed to keep as many people as possible safe, secure and healthy? Or predatory ideas, designed to further enrich the already unimaginably wealthy while leaving the most vulnerable further exposed?'[4]

Suddenly, since the coronavirus lockdown began in March 2020, none of this sounds too far-fetched or nearly as radical. Spain announced a roll out of universal basic income[5] and Amsterdam embraced the Doughnut economics model as proposed by Kate Raworth, aiming to be 'a thriving, regenerative and inclusive city for all citizens, while respecting the planetary boundaries'.[6]

Both the Doughnut economics model and the Convivial Conservation are spatial practices. Büscher and Fletcher envision a landscape, urban or rural, 'wherein important species could live … by identifying and studying economic and political impediments and opportunities related to potential spatial implications of solving human–animal conflicts in these spaces'.[7]

As the crisis saw universities move to teaching online, it is important to reflect on ideas and methods used in architectural education. However, more importantly, as educators we should be asking ourselves: What future will our former students imagine? In other words: What have we been teaching our students so far? What future will they shape for all of us with the tools we equipped them with?

The following text looks at student projects created in the Ecosystem City Studio, a part of the masters programme at the Sheffield School of Architecture in 2018 and 2019. The examples highlight the power of architectural education as an effective and transformative practice with a potential to reach far beyond university walls.

The polyphonic city

We are the Ecosystem City Studio, one of the design studios at the Sheffield School of Architecture. The key question we were trying to answer was what it means to be an architect when the world is – literally – burning. The site for our design explorations was situated between two post-industrial neighbourhoods in Sheffield, on a piece of overgrown land criss-crossed by paths leading to the canal and a disused railway line.

We are observing the post-industrial city and discover that a lot of what the Industrial Revolution left in Sheffield was taken over by nature. The area along the Don River and the canal is a diverse ecosystem thriving among the remnants of Sheffield's industrial past. Here, at the canal, close to the city centre and next to a big roundabout, it is possible to spot herons, kingfishers and cranes, not long ago otters moved in and there is a buzz about salmon in the river. They are all welcome and their presence is greeted with excitement. However, what about buddleia, the hardy plant, which takes over ruins and together with equally stubborn lichens, mosses and ferns, dwells even on brick walls of the open tunnels where trains cross the city? What about grey squirrels replacing the local reds? Which organisms are worthy of our protection and care, and which should be eradicated? What is the difference between otters and rats? From a biological point of view, all those 'intruders' and 'pests', are simply very successful urban species. Should we punish them for that?

We are listening to the city and it speaks to us with many voices. We find a frame for our perspective at Mikhail Bakhtin's idea of polyphony. In the city, human and non-human voices are constantly engaged in a dialogue, negotiating their place in the world, entwined in complex networks of interdependence. We start with a question of what lives in the city next to us, and to our surprise we learn that cities are often the islands of biodiversity in the sea of cultivated agricultural land hostile to life beyond tightly controlled crops. Our point of view is shifting as we become aware of the potential of all those in-between, leftover, forgotten, abandoned and inaccessible urban spaces. They are often nature's first footholds in the long campaign to establish her kingdom. We learn that every ecosystem aims to reach its stable peak, but it is a long perspective, a process spanning lifetimes, and therefore imperceptible from our short-lived human point of view.

Sanjukta Jitendhar, axonometric view of the proposal on site. Student project, Ecosystem City Studio, SSoA, 2018/19.

Our theoretical point of departure was the Anthropocene, the idea that a new geological era marked by human activity had started. However, we soon realise that the Anthropocene does not serve us well, because of its human-centred bias. We entertain the idea that from the perspective of the planet it would be better if humanity disappeared to let damaged ecosystems recover, perhaps making space for a new, non-human civilisation to take over.

In 2002, Paul Crutzen, the same scientist who argued for the introduction of the geological new era, proposed big-scale geoengineering projects to optimise the climate as a response to the havoc wreaked by humans. We are suspicious of such grand gestures and do not trust technology enough to rely on it to solve such complicated problems as the climate crisis. Human hubris – or to be precise, 'humans' standing here for usually white male and Western scientists – makes us reject this perspective and search for other voices.

We choose to pay attention to what is overlooked and undervalued, we uncover what is invisible and underrated, and try to listen to other voices. It becomes apparent that dichotomies are of no use for us: urban/rural, natural/artificial, human/non-human, none of those binary classifications help us understand and describe the world. Cities spill into suburbs and then dissolve into even more undefined urbanised areas. There is no true wilderness left on the planet and the city community does not only consist of humans, as it includes all species sharing the city space with us. This expanded perspective forces us to ask the question what would happen if we flattened the hierarchies, knocked humans from their pedestal of the measure of all things and gave voice to all living organisms.

If the very survival of our civilisation is under threat, we also need to ask the question of what keeps it alive. Feminist theory explains that all those every day, ubiquitous – therefore almost invisible – gestures of care, usually associated with women's work, keep our world turning. Support networks, emotional labour, collectives and cooperatives, without which the status quo cannot be maintained and without which no change is possible. They are the laborious, yet often surprisingly creative gestures of care: fixing, mending, cleaning, repairing … . No bridge is meant to last forever, entropy patiently nibbles on matter, the proverbial drop hollows concrete. What is complex, must become unstable, the simplicity of the matter's basic building blocks is the ultimate end we all – human, non-human, alive and non-living – will eventually meet.

Sanjukta Jitendhar. The process of programme generation is driven by care on a personal level, care for others and care for things. Student project, Ecosystem City Studio, SSoA, 2018/19.

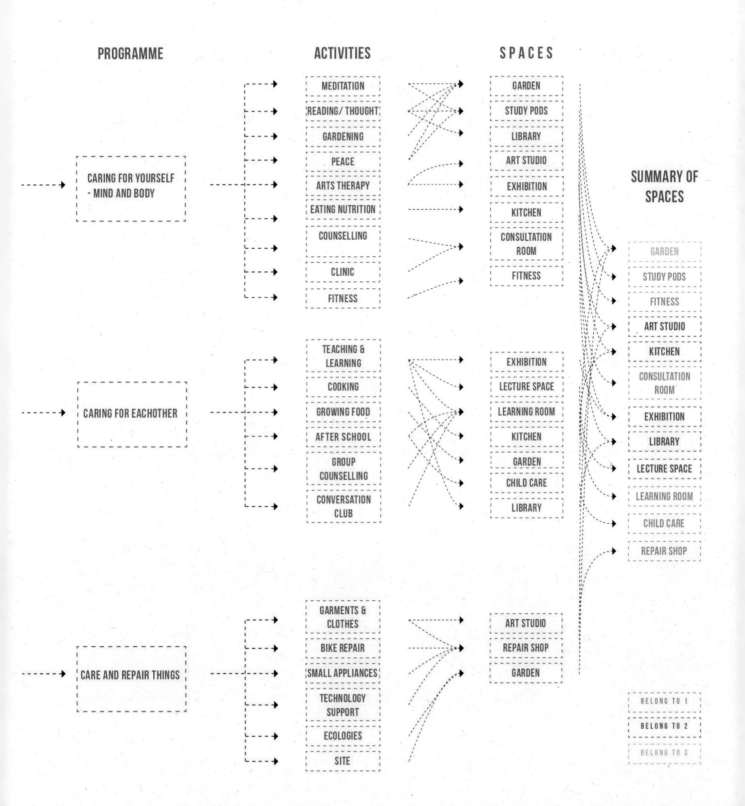

PROGRAMME ACTIVITIES SPACES

CARING FOR YOURSELF - MIND AND BODY

MEDITATION
READING/ THOUGHT
GARDENING
PEACE
ARTS THERAPY
EATING NUTRITION
COUNSELLING
CLINIC
FITNESS

GARDEN
STUDY PODS
LIBRARY
ART STUDIO
EXHIBITION
KITCHEN
CONSULTATION ROOM
FITNESS

SUMMARY OF SPACES

GARDEN
STUDY PODS
FITNESS
ART STUDIO
KITCHEN
CONSULTATION ROOM
EXHIBITION
LIBRARY
LECTURE SPACE
LEARNING ROOM
CHILD CARE
REPAIR SHOP

CARING FOR EACHOTHER

TEACHING & LEARNING
COOKING
GROWING FOOD
AFTER SCHOOL
GROUP COUNSELLING
CONVERSATION CLUB

EXHIBITION
LECTURE SPACE
LEARNING ROOM
KITCHEN
GARDEN
CHILD CARE
LIBRARY

CARE AND REPAIR THINGS

GARMENTS & CLOTHES
BIKE REPAIR
SMALL APPLIANCES
TECHNOLOGY SUPPORT
ECOLOGIES
SITE

ART STUDIO
REPAIR SHOP
GARDEN

BELONG TO 1
BELONG TO 2
BELONG TO 3

Right: Sanjukta Jitendhar, the most prominent space in the project is a quiet space for (breast) feeding. This design gesture celebrates the activity, one that is very rarely given appropriate space and attention, and elevates it to status of the most important space in the building. Student project, Ecosystem City Studio, SSoA, 2018/19.

Left: Sanjukta Jitendhar, interior of the (breast)feeding space. Student project, Ecosystem City Studio, SSoA, 2018/19.

Architecture and the Climate Emergency

In architecture it is not only the calculation of the maintenance costs or the longevity of materials. It is also a seemingly trivial issue of how to clean the windows and who will have to kneel on the bathroom floor while trying to clean an inaccessible nook behind the toilet. It is the question of the distance a granite slab will travel before it is fixed on the elevation, as well as who is the user and the client, and what if they are not the same person and have contradictory interests? How can an architect find herself in such a situation, and how far is she willing to move the boundaries of her ethical and professional responsibility so that she can look herself in the mirror without shame?

Stephen Graham and Nigel Thrift write that architects rarely take into consideration the maintenance of the building in the design process.[8] There are still buildings designed without anyone, throughout the design and construction process, considering the need to clean the windows.[9]

We keep searching. According to Jason W. Moore it is not the human activity as such to be blamed for the climate emergency, but capitalism and its logic of plunder and constant growth. If we assume this position, and following Moore define the new era as the Capitalocene, the only possible answer, however daunting and ambitious, would be to think of an alternative to capitalism.

Design responses

Sanjukta Jitendhar, a final year masters student, does exactly that and challenges capitalism with the help of the feminist methodology of care in her diploma project. She uses three modes of care as her starting points, which follow:
1. Care for yourself.
2. Care for each other.
3. Care for things.
Her project imagines anti-capitalist architecture and asks if it would help us imagine a better, more just and equitable world.[10]

Care is embedded in her design process at every stage, as demonstrated in her programme generation process. She extends care to what lives on the site and who lives next to it, she cares about the neighbourhood and the city, about the organisation of the construction process, and she cares about people who in turn will be taking care of the building in the future.

Her project focuses on a civic building, a centre of care for local residents, mainly stay-at-home mothers from once flourishing and now neglected neighbourhoods. In this project, following Joan C. Tronto and Berenice Fisher, care is understood as '… everything that we do to maintain, continue, and repair 'our world' so that we can live in it as well as possible. That world includes our bodies, ourselves, and our environment, all of which we seek to interweave in a complex, life sustaining web.'[11]

The architecture of the building elevates care-giving as the most spatially celebrated room in the building as a quiet space for (breast)feeding.

Another example is a diploma project by Isabelle Chamberlayne. She defines the aims of the Ecosystem City Studio as: 'Using polyphony, Ecosystem City will aim to redefine our cities as platforms for the expression of all living organisms to ultimately develop new environmentally sustainable models of rich coexistence.'[12] She proposes intergenerational social housing interacting with the urban wild.

A neighbourhood at the canal blending into the urban edgelands[13] has already been taken over by nature. The idea of the carnivalesque, as proposed by Mikhail Bakhtin, here defined as a celebration of the unexpected encounter with the non-human other, is one of the design drivers in the project. Chamberlayne asks: 'Considering that architecture historically reflected the proportions of the Vitruvian Man, seen as the definition of universal beauty, what would the architecture that de-centres human power structures look like?'[14]

The polyphonic design method is a deeply ethical approach. Within this framework, the architect must define herself in the relationship to the other human and non-human.

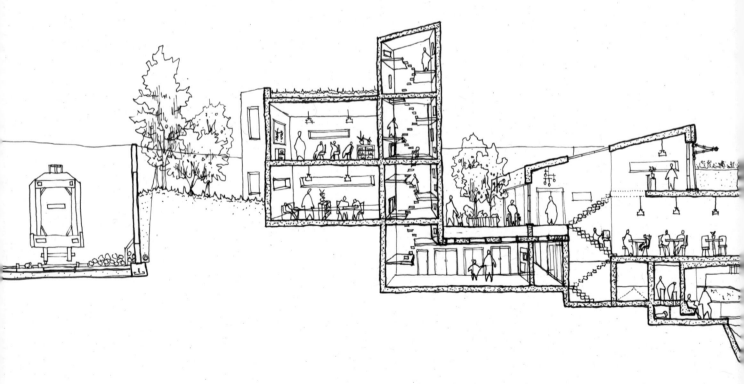

Her answer is a space of adventure, discovery and delight inspired by free-range childhood. Humans and non-humans live close to each other, where opportunities for chance encounters are carefully curated through landscape design and small architectural gestures to increase their probability.

A project by first year masters student Alice Howland, entitled 'Ottertecture', proposes a children's activity and education centre for the Canal River Trust. The surface of the walls is specifically designed to encourage the growth of ferns and mosses, which would gradually cover the building and hide it in the landscape. Carefully designed nooks in the elevation facing the canal offer the type of spaces favoured by otters. It is possible to climb the walls and roofs of the building, and penetrate it through a series of passages that offer a non-human perspective, challenging the default human perception of space.

This is architecture that aims to educate as it facilitates the exploration of the world through experience of non-human points of view. In this space, children are encouraged to crawl, climb and touch the moss, stroke the ferns, play hide-and-seek and, if they are lucky, catch a glimpse of an otter tail in the water. Here humans can encounter and interact with non-human others, and experience the world from a different point of view.

The carnivalesque landscape and 'Ottertecture' are both inspired by edgelands and their potential. These two projects share the childlike wonder and use the child's point of view as a design tool to open the space for new perspectives and accommodate more voices.

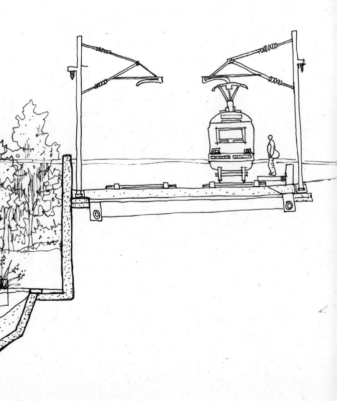

Alice Howland, 'Ottertecture', section with proposed otter holts on the other side of the canal and otter-friendly spaces embedded in the canal-facing part of the building. The project caters for an existing otter population at the Sheffield Canal and enhances chances for human-animal encounters. Student project, Ecosystem City Studio, SSoA, 2018/19.

Polyphony and radical inclusivity

The polyphonic design method is a deeply ethical approach. Within this framework, the architect must define herself in the relationship to the other human and non-human. It is a narrative of constant questioning of the status quo and the role of the architect in the world. It is not possible to hide behind the pretence of objectivism and modernist faith in one, rational and universal order. It is also not possible to be seduced by postmodern multiplication of narratives, although the questioning of the strong subject is the basis of this method.

The Anthropocene and Capitalocene put humans on the pedestal and in the centre of events, reducing all other living creatures to a merely reactive position. However, nothing ever happens in a vacuum, we are interconnected with others by multiple bounds. 'We are at stake to each other,'[15] writes Donna Haraway. She flattens hierarchies and braids them back into linear, multispecies, tentacular assemblages of the curiously named Chthulucene. In this perspective, we would form multi-species alliances to survive the crisis.

This is the kind of subjectivity that gets our attention, a subjectivity which is '... always contextual, never a closed whole, it exists more like a node/ compression than as a separate entity'.[16] It constitutes the idea of Radical Inclusivity, which in architecture is defined as '... a possibility to use the building in various ways, by various users, human and not human actors. Every element of infrastructure which serves an egoistic interest of a building can also work for others and therefore participate in creating of the common good. Building walls become then "interfaces" mediating between what is private and what is shared. Synergy and cooperation become the key rules. All buildings, including privately owned, become interfaces and elements of social infrastructure.'[17]

Laboratories of change

The world is burning, even if the cities during lockdown seemed eerily quiet and empty. We were delighted to observe animals venturing into cities, curious and unbothered, freely roaming the empty streets. It was a deceptively bucolic vision, blink and it was gone, a mere dream to cherish before the cars returned to the roads. However, it does not mean we should accept the world will eventually come back to the so-called normal, where we were senselessly burning fossil fuels, encroaching on the biodiverse areas and coming into contact with wild animals which most likely gave us COVID-19 in return.

We should not abandon hope, because architects have something unique to offer. As the new, post-pandemic world emerges, design studios in architecture schools have a chance to not only imagine new possibilities and ask questions, but also to shape answers. We can be the collaborative laboratories of change, producing and testing ideas in space, precisely because of our privileged position where we are free to experiment and question.

This is what we will have to offer to the post-coronavirus world: our ability to produce and test ideas in space, to work collaboratively with other disciplines. Our toolbox contains a set of unique skills in making connections, understanding networks and complex processes, and all this – in space. Someone has to re-imagine how we work, travel, relax and live. This is our time to claim our seat at the table and contribute to the shaping of the new world. Our task is to make sure that there are plenty of ideas lying around.

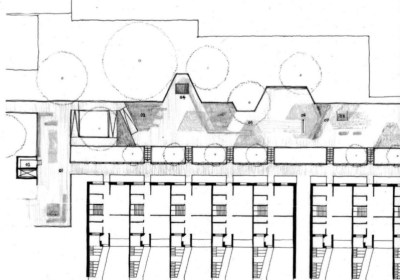

Isabelle Chamberlayne, intergenerational housing, plan with landscaping. Student project, Ecosystem City Studio, SSoA, 2018/19.

What have we been teaching our students so far? What future will they shape for all of us with the tools we equipped them with?

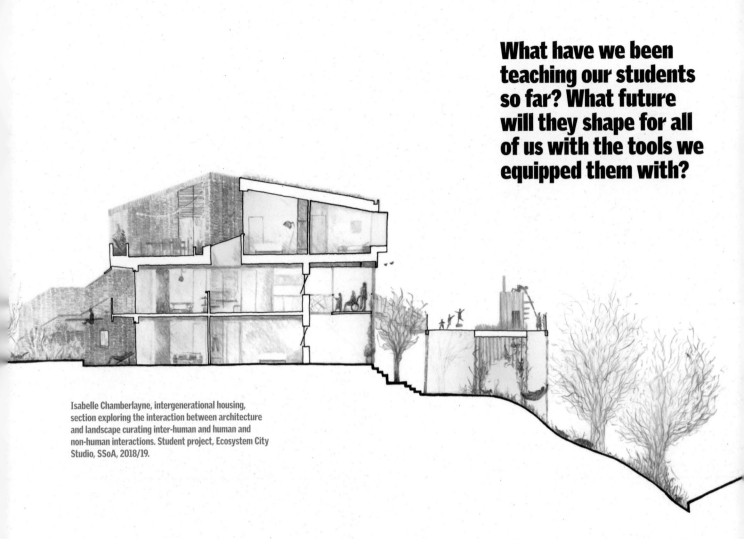

Isabelle Chamberlayne, intergenerational housing, section exploring the interaction between architecture and landscape curating inter-human and human and non-human interactions. Student project, Ecosystem City Studio, SSoA, 2018/19.

1 Friedman, M., Capitalism and Freedom: Fortieth Anniversary Edition, *University of Chicago Press*, Chicago, 2002, p. xiv.

2 Büscher, B. & Fletcher, R., *The Conservation Revolution. Radical Ideas for Saving Nature beyond the Anthropocene*, Verso, London, 2020.

3 'Democracy Now', *Coronavirus Capitalism: Naomi Klein's Case for Transformative Change Amid Coronavirus Pandemic*, https://www.democracynow.org/2020/3/19/naomi_klein_coronavirus_capitalism, accessed 10 April 2020.

4 Ibid.

5 Ng, K., 'Coronavirus: Spain to become first country in Europe to roll out universal basic income', *Independent*, 6 April 2020, https://www.independent.co.uk/news/world/europe/coronavirus-spain-universal-basic-income-europe-a9449336.html, accessed 10 April 2020.

6 Raworth, K., 'The Amsterdam City Doughnut. A tool for transformative action', *Doughnut Economics*, https://www.kateraworth.com/wp/wp-content/

uploads/2020/04/20200406-AMS-portrait-EN-Single-page-web-420x210mm.pdf, accessed 10 April 2020.

7 Büscher, B. & Fletcher, R., *The Conservation Revolution. Radical Ideas for Saving Nature beyond the Anthropocene*, Verso, London, 2020, p. 192.

8 Graham, S. & Thrift, N., 'Out of Order Understanding Repair and Maintenance', *Theory, Culture & Society*, 24, no. 3, 2007, pp. 1–25.

9 The COVID-19 pandemic has brought the issues of maintenance and hygiene into sharp focus as they quickly became a matter of public safety. The pandemic also highlighted a wider issue of key workers being not only routinely undervalued despite their crucial role, but also unprotected during the pandemic and therefore paying the ultimate price for our collective blind spot.

10 The project was awarded the Blue Riband Award at the Blueprint for the Future exhibition in London in July 2019. Blueprint, 366, pp. 88–89.

11 Tronto, J. & Fisher, B., 'Toward a Feminist Theory of Caring' in *Circles of Care*, eds E. Abel & M. Nelson, SUNY Press, New York, 1990, pp. 36–54.

12 Chamberlayne, I., *Design Manifesto* (2019), unpublished, Sheffield School of Architecture.

13 Farley, P. & Roberts, M.S., *Edgelands*, Vintage Books, London, 2012.

14 Ibid.

15 Haraway, D., 'Tentacular Thinking: Anthropocene, Capitalocene, Chthulucene', *e-flux Journal*, #75, 2016, https://www.e-flux.com/journal/75/67125/tentacular-thinking-anthropocene-capitalocene-chthulucene/, accessed 10 April 2020.

16 This definition of the subject is used by Krzysztof Nawratek and his idea of Radical Inclusivity. Nawratek K., 'Poza wspólnotę – budując to, co wspólne', *Autoportret*, nr 51 [4], 2015, https://autoportret.pl/artykuly/poza-wspolnote-budujac-to-co-wspolne/, accessed 10 April 2020, translated from Polish by Kasia Nawratek.

17 Nawratek, K. & Nawratek, K, 'On the Frustrating Impossibility of Inclusive Architecture', in *Radical Inclusivity. Architecture and Urbanism*, ed. K. Nawratek, Barcelona, DPR-Barcelona, 2015, p. 23.

PROFILE:
Towards a Zero Carbon Architecture
Mikhail Riches

Clay Field, Suffolk, UK;
Goldsmith Street, Norwich, UK;
Housing for the City of York, UK

Right: Mikhail Riches, Clay Field, Suffolk, 2009. Older children's kickabout area with the staggered terraces behind. Hempcrete walls are finished with lime render and are limewashed in typical Suffolk colours.

Left: Small children's play area under an orchard of local pear and apple trees. This forms the heart of the Clay Field scheme. Kitchen windows and front doors look directly over for easy natural surveillance.

Below: Houses are arranged in terraces of three. They are arranged around the site to minimise overshadowing each other and create views through. Communal spaces include a wildflower meadow, a small children's play area and shared allotments.

From the Clay Field project in Suffolk, a passive solar scheme built out of timber, hemp and lime, to the Passivhaus Goldsmith Street housing in Norwich, London-based architecture practice Mikhail Riches continue to explore, learn and develop in low-energy construction. With current housing projects for local authorities in York and Somerset at the time of writing, the practice is planning a route map towards zero carbon, both for energy in use and embodied carbon. The following building profiles take us through some of Mikhail Riches' key projects from the practices' perspective.

Clay Field, Suffolk

Clay Field provides 22 affordable family houses and four flats in a Suffolk village. Built for Orwell Housing Association and the Suffolk Preservation Society, following an RIBA competition in 2005, the scheme aspires to a low-maintenance durability and gentle minimalist ecology. Thanks to an ambitious client brief, we were encouraged to explore a 'deep green' approach, both in terms of future resource use and in embodied carbon.

Accommodation is arranged in terraces of three, positioned in distinctive groups around three communal gardens: a wildflower meadow, allotments and a playground in an orchard. Terraces are laid out in a staggered pattern, to avoid overshadowing. Each terrace is back-to-back with another, with the lower two-storey terrace to the south and low profile roofs are sculpted to optimise sunlight penetration.

We explored the use of very low-embodied energy materials, with unusual sprayed hempcrete construction in a panelised timber frame, with finishes of rough sawn cedar, with limewashed lime render in Suffolk colours. Garden walls are laid with unfired clay blocks, lime rendered and protected by a 'roof' of cedar shingles. A shared woodchip biomass boiler, rainwater recycling and whole house ventilation serves each house.

A small children's play area is located at the heart of the scheme, overlooking a bigger kickabout area, which was given swales, drained and planted with willow.

Sustainability engineers on the project, Buro Happold, funded its own post-occupancy analysis, which made for fascinating reading and initial results varied hugely from house to house. Further research was commissioned, interviewing residents directly, and we learnt there was a significant performance gap in some areas. For example, there were unexpected heat losses across the biomass district heating system, different homes had varied energy and resource use profiles, and the communal rainwater collection had led to anxiety and occasional over-use. Positive feedback included heating bills for residents being low – even lower than predicted – and the area for growing vegetables had helped start a residents' association.

The main takeaway from Clay Field was that if a site can accommodate a true solar strategy with midwinter sun to primary windows whilst making a convincing place of utility, durability and beauty, the approach could be applied to any residential project.

Above: Mikhail Riches, Clay Field, Suffolk, 2009. Hempcrete offered a low carbon building material and was spread into a prefabricated timber frame on site.

Goldsmith Street, Norwich

In 2008 Norwich City Council ran an RIBA competition to find an architect to support its vision to set a benchmark for its affordable housing development plans. Emulating the sought-after nineteenth-century 'Golden Triangle' nearby, where terraces are laid out with a separation of only 14m, Goldsmith Street demonstrates how to achieve sustainable low-rise, high-density living. With a shared vision to create a low-energy development, the scheme was masterplanned around these principles from the outset to make best use of solar access and combat fuel poverty for residents. Annual energy costs are estimated to be 70% less than for the average household.

Streets are set out so that main elevations face south and benefit from winter gains, whilst windows are designed with solar shading to prevent summer overheating. Roof pitches are modelled to avoid overshadowing in winter and internal layouts configured so that the majority of habitable rooms face south. Intuitive placemaking sits at its heart, with the back gardens of the central terraces sharing a secure ginnel (alleyway) for children to play together, and a wide landscaped walkway for the community runs directly through the middle of the development. Roads have been designed in such a way that cars travel slowly, with safe crossing points located throughout the scheme in the form of raised tables.

Following the initial stages of the design process, the client challenged us to achieve full Passivhaus certification for all units. Fortunately, having optimised the site layout for solar access, this was achieved with only minor design changes.

Architecture and the Climate Emergency

Our proposed configuration enabled us to counter some of the negative perceptions of Passivhaus. For example, we were able to introduce relatively large north-facing living room windows.

Impeccable detailing was required to meet the exacting standards of Passivhaus, with even the smallest details considered. Letterboxes are built into external porches to reduce any possibility of draughts and perforated aluminium brise-soleils provide sun shading above windows and doors.

Passivhaus design focuses on a 'fabric-first' approach to construction, which ensures that energy demand is reduced as a priority whilst still providing high levels of comfort (summer and winter) and maintaining excellent air quality. To achieve this low heating demand, incredibly high levels of air tightness, thermal insulation and high-quality triple-glazed windows are used to reduce heat loss. A balanced mechanical ventilation system is used in conjunction with this to provide a high level of indoor air quality, assist with summer comfort and minimise ventilation heat losses.

These elements all work together to ensure the energy demand for heating is only 12 kW/m^2/year, with no requirement for renewable energy generation. The materials lifecycle of Goldsmith Street is anywhere from 60 to 100 years, with the timber frame structure and panels of the project reducing the significant end of life disposal issues faced with more traditional brick and block construction methods. The majority of materials (timber, brick, cellulose insulation, clay roof tiles) within the project allow for reuse or recycling at the end of life stage of the development.

The analysis for whole life embodied carbon shows that over the lifetime of the development (60/100 years) a total of 11.21/6.73 $KgCO_2eq/m^2$ (with a further 1065.6/1776 $KgCO_2eq/m^2$ over those 60/100 years based on the current services system) would be produced.

Below: Mikhail Riches, Goldsmith Street, Norwich, 2016. Goldsmith Street is a scheme of 14m wide streets, a scale inspired by local Edwardian housing.

Above: Mikhail Riches, Goldsmith Street, Norwich, 2016. The back gardens of the central terraces share a secure ginnel for children to play together safely.

Housing for the City of York

The City of York Council declared a climate emergency in March 2019, shortly after its newly formed Housing Delivery Programme released the tender for its new house-building programme. Following a two-stage design submission, Mikhail Riches was appointed framework provider.

The council's ambitions were clear from the outset: new homes in York must be beautiful, healthy and sustainable at both house and neighbourhood level, building on and extending the legacy of York's rich history of pioneering house-building.

Developed at the beginning of the programme, York's Design Manual acts as a strategic brief and sets out key environmental targets. All new homes must be designed and built to certified Passivhaus standards and the developments are to achieve zero carbon.

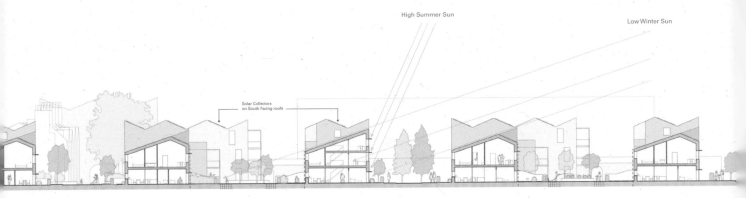

High Summer Sun

Low Winter Sun

Solar Collectors
on South Facing roofs

We knew how to approach Passivhaus. Reaching zero carbon is more challenging. It is vital to clarify zero carbon during the briefing phase of projects, setting a definition for the wider project team to work towards. The following has been set at York, backed by the Executive Member for Housing, Green Party, Councillor Craghill, who stated: 'We were inspired by what was achieved at Goldsmith Street. Passivhaus provides an excellent fabric-first approach that closes the performance gap and ensures energy demand is very low. However, we wanted to go further. Our 450 beautiful Passivhaus-certified homes across the city in zero carbon neighbourhoods will also promote sustainable transport, good use of green space and a sense of community. Each development will generate at least as much energy as each home requires.'

Passivhaus provides an excellent baseline to achieve zero carbon, a fabric-first approach that closes the performance gap and truly reduces energy demand.

A number of different strategies are being considered for heating and hot water, including air source heat pumps, ground source heat pumps and solar thermal electric (i.e. no gas). All these will be combined with photovoltaics for on-site generation, offsetting the site-wide energy consumption.

The design team is carefully balancing the appropriateness of these different systems for houses and flats, considering capital costs, maintenance and user interface. Key to this development is not only how these services perform but also how they are integrated into the wider development without affecting the quality of public realm, private and shared amenity spaces.

Understanding the relative impact embodied carbon has on reaching the RIBA's 2030 zero carbon target, Mikhail Riches is currently developing a strategy to measure, report and share the embodied carbon levels of our projects in York.

Previously relying on knowledge, intuition and research to reduce embodied carbon through material choices, we now want to enhance this with quantitative analysis to understand and improve

Mikhail Riches, council housing estate, York, ongoing. Section of proposals for Ordnance Lane in York. Like Goldsmith Street, terraces face south, minimising overshadowing of neighbours and allowing for affordable Passivhaus certification for the building fabric. Targeting zero carbon, the scheme also provides photovoltaics on roofs and air source heat pumps.

upon our design process. Material recycling and exploration of reuse and refurb options will also contribute to our process of lowering embodied carbon.

We believe that zero carbon targets should be reinforced with design that promotes a reduced carbon lifestyle. The mixed tenure developments in York will encourage reduced car use, cycling, neighbourly relationships, communal food growing and intergenerational living.

Conclusion

Ideally, central government would go further with more robust regulations and to find ways to encourage timber construction, but we take heart that local authorities are now the trailblazers, setting challenging targets driven by their climate emergency declarations, and we enjoy working with them to realise these ambitions. Once again, local authority housing is leading the way, both in the provision of much needed homes and as importantly in addressing climate change and setting an example of exemplary low-carbon developments for others to emulate.

Mikhail Riches, council housing estate, York, ongoing. Communal gardens with a 20-m separation are shared by residents, with opportunities for a secure children's play area and spaces for socialising and for growing food.

dRMM, Kingsdale School, London, UK, rebuilt from 2004–07. Music performance room, a perforated timber 'music box' built in 2006. Full size CLT panels ensured no waste. All window cut-outs became furniture.

PROFILE:
Radical Sustainable Architecture
Alex de Rijke
dRMM

Kingsdale School, London, UK

We shape our buildings; thereafter they shape us. Winston Churchill

Kingsdale School was a ground-breaking education architecture project featuring several design innovations, including a mixed-use social/education space together with pioneering sustainable materials and techniques. Designs were developed following a year-long consultation process to develop the brief with staff, students, parents and neighbours. Alex de Rijke of dRMM explains the design process and development of the school.

Kingsdale School, London

Thousands of sustainable design decisions were made by dRMM in the 2000–09 project for the transformation of Kingsdale School, a post-war steel-framed, glass-clad London school campus. Now it is cited as an ecological and material design 'exemplar' for new school architecture, and also for radical re-use or rather than replacement of obsolete building stock. At the time, we mainly thought of it as an holistic design demonstration for children (and teachers) who were bored of their school and needed inspiration.

The Kingsdale School transformation started as an Architecture Foundation (AF) competition project and became a government-backed precursor to the Building Schools for the Future programme. The AF saw the 'SchoolWorks' pioneer project as an opportunity to demonstrate that school architecture could positively influence pupil performance. dRMM relished this challenge, embracing the opportunity to experiment and simultaneously demonstrate how architecture influences the wider environment. Kingsdale School was chosen because:
· it was a poor state school in a rich area
· it had a 'failing school' reputation
· the head was progressive and willing to host the experiment in order to deservedly improve the school environment.

The word 'environment' became the mantra of our design team and was used as an inclusive term, encompassing the natural, built and social environments of the school. These definitions in turn sit within extended contexts of the world, the city and the community respectively. The design team was aware that its various responsibilities had many repercussions throughout this interwoven dynamic.

An early decision was not to follow the expected solution to demolish the highly problematic post-war school after building a new one alongside it. Although for the staff, students and neighbours the unpopular 1950s school was variously an 'eyesore', too hot, too cold, too cramped and they wanted a new school, dRMM chose to re-use and recycle, adapt and dramatically transform the existing structure, adding key elements to this and the wider campus. This was partly practical

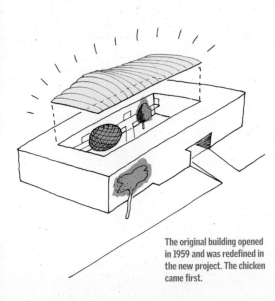

The original building opened in 1959 and was redefined in the new project. The chicken came first.

expedience to provide bigger and better spaces by extending the old rather than a new school building built to contemporary codes, partly not wanting to waste the existing material fabric – the steel structure alone was already carbon-heavy – and partly not wishing to erase but build on its history. Retrofit as a commitment to the controversial school was not only about avoiding waste of material and energy, it was about social sustainability. It was a way of reversing prejudices against Kingsdale, the 'bad' or 'ugly' state school building with its largely black underprivileged community, coincidentally situated in a privileged white area, and next door to one of the most successful private school in London, Dulwich College. Retrofit became a process of commitment to Kingsdale School's past, as well as its future, an environmental and cultural responsibility jointly taken between the design team and school management.

Despite our informed respect for LCC Chief Architect Sir Leslie Martin's 'Clasp' post-war design, Kingsdale School's institutionalised grid of Modernist architectural devices, Cartesian geometry and purist composition, thin envelope and lack of insulation, endless corridor circulation and single aspect classrooms, uniformity of spaces and strict segregation of uses was all carefully and methodically attacked. Together with creative (limited) demolition, our design strategy deployed:

· different forms, geometries, materials and colours to the existing palette
· smart systems with natural heating, venting and lighting
· introduced radically different spatial experiences.

The rule of thumb was to transform by intervention and addition, but with the minimum material to the maximum effect and holistic benefit.

A good example of this approach was a new roof over the old building. The design exploits the potential of the existing building, superimposing an ETFE roof over two internal courtyards connected to become a 36 x 72 x 15 m space, through the demolition of the old hall. The new roof structure was light enough to stand on the existing school top floor steel frame rather than requiring foundations. The 'reduction' of the existing building mass in favour of creating space had many advantages beyond the obvious benefit of creating a very

A lightweight translucent membrane spans the entire school quad; the first 'variable skin' ETFE roof offers controllable solar gain.

Cross-section through existing school wings connected by superimposed ETFE enclosure creates a large multi-purpose atrium with a controllable micro-climate.

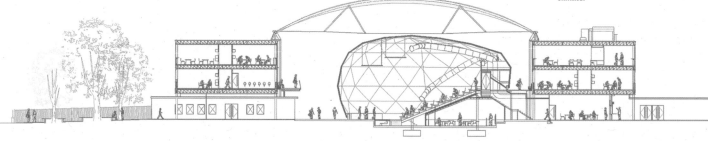

Architecture and the Climate Emergency

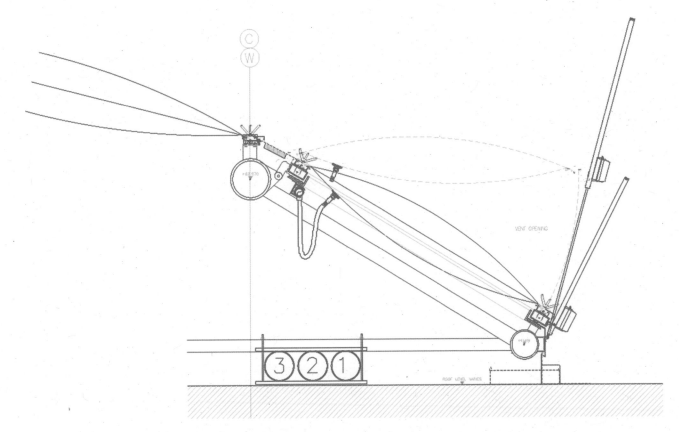

Detail of atrium ventilation
system at existing building roof
level. Perimeter ETFE roof vents
operated by sensors expel hot
air using the Venturi effect. Cool
air is drawn in at ground level.

large mixed-use volume without recourse to new foundations or facades, or any mechanical heating, cooling or ventilation requirement.

The new roof over the courtyard significantly increased internal floor area whilst reducing external surface area; a single insulating membrane replacing four largely uninsulated glass external walls. Spring/autumn heat loss from the single-glazed classroom windows was captured and re-used to contribute to the heating of the new enclosed courtyard, along with passive solar gain controlled by the 'variable skin' ETFE roof. The previous summer term problem of major heat gains through the formerly external glass facades, resulting in almost unusable classrooms, was thus overcome without having to touch the facade fabric. A way of understanding this approach to energy and usable space is that the addition of the inflatable ETFE roof could be described as making 'inhabitable triple glazing'.

The 'inside/outside' space thus created as if under the sky hosts a timber music performance/cinema auditorium, a 1,200+ student assembly area, and a dining area cool enough to 'chill' in, together with flexible areas for groups, exhibitions, and so on. Aerial walkways, a bridge, a lift and stairs make new and faster circulation connections, allowing the previous ring of corridors to be shortened, removed or adapted to other uses.

Kingsdale School already had a long and proud history of achievement in music and sport. For this reason, other subject departments in need of an improved environment were given priority attention and reconstruction phases of this nine-year transformation project.

In the existing school campus, both music and sports facilities were separate from the central main building, respectively sited in inadequate and undersized satellite buildings near the perimeter. When the budget was finally allocated to these facilities, it was decided to combine the departments in order to make a proposed single new development more efficient, cost-effective and sustainable – aspects that often go hand in hand.

dRMM thereby made a case for the first public 100% cross-laminated timber building in the UK, an early application showcasing engineered timber's capacity to meet all construction and environmental criteria. Additional to the then novel ideological argument for carbon storage, key practical advantages lay in exploiting modern prefabrication methods inherent to CLT manufacture and fast assembly on site. As at the time (2006) this was unprecedented in Britain, it required holistic cost analysis and translation of European safety standards, as well as the satisfaction of central government funding the project, Local Authority Planning and Building Control (Southwark), London Fire Brigade and Zurich insurance.

A design was conceived of two independent volumes connected by a shared entrance and core; a transparent link inviting entry between relatively closed timber boxes. The entry point also creates new access to the rest of the school campus from the perimeter in order to encourage community use, particularly from the adjacent housing estate and primary school. The sports hall and music department together form a 'gatehouse' to the school site; a boundary but more than a fence.

Sports halls are necessarily single volumes, large and high, as defined by pitch layouts and DfES and Sport England guidelines. The design challenge for Kingsdale Sports Hall was to provide an economic CLT box charged with daylight and expressive architecture. A rectangular open plan with hyperbolic curved roof offered a simple footprint with clerestory windows and spectacular space – high enough for a freestanding services/changing room 'building' within the hall. By contrast, and for acoustic reasons, the music department was designed as a wedge-shaped angular cellular plan, perforated with many small openings lighting the various separated soundproofed rooms. dRMM modelled many options for curvature generated from straight elements to establish the most beautiful and efficient form to be made from standard timber beams and flat panels. The sculptural geometry of the sports hall's 'hyperbolic paraboloid' roof and the

Sports Hall under construction 2006 – the UK's first CLT building. A 100% timber, column-free, highly insulated building features natural light, ventilation and finishes.

The previously external courtyard, shown hosting the school's 60th anniversary celebrations in 2019. The ETFE 'variable skin' roof provides 3,200 m² of naturally lit/ heated/ventilated open space containing tress, plants and the timber auditorium.

Project credits:
Professional collaborations included working with:
Gordon Cowley on a timber geodesic auditorium
Michael Hadi/MHA engineers and KLH on the Music and Sports complex – the first CLT buildings in the UK
Andy Ford/Fulcrum with Ben Morris/Vector on the world's first ETFE solar control roof
Joep van Lieshout/AVL on 'useful art'.

music school 'wedge', together with inventive cladding details, creates simultaneously large and small internal/external scales with intriguing perspective. The loadbearing, solid CLT construction system offers structure and internal finish as one process, requiring only external woodfibre insulation and profiled weatherproof cladding – a didactic construction demonstration.

It could be argued that the transformed Kingsdale School presents itself as a 3D lesson in building long-term sustainability. Extending the life of the existing building resulted in the largest space ever created in a British school, a massively useful asset. Together with the all-timber construction of the auditorium, sports hall and music blocks, and their respective low carbon construction and low energy systems, the quality of daylight and deliberately uplifting architecture all combine to de-institutionalise the education environment. The intention to encourage learning to happen between classes and beyond the curriculum is difficult to measure but the act of rebuilding also had the effect – during construction and onwards – of rebuilding morale amongst staff and students. With the improved architecture, pride, grades and recruitment have improved beyond recognition.

Helen & Hard,
Vindmøllebakken,
Stavanger, Norway, 2019.
Half-climatised hallway
around which the main
shared facilities are
gathered: workshop,
laundry, lounge, co-work
space, guest room and the
central communal space.

PROFILE:
Co-housing Project
Siv Helene
Stangeland

Vindmøllebakken,
Stavanger, Norway

Axonometry of a Gaining
by Sharing co-housing
showing the four gains:
economic gain by
reduced m2 and sharing,
social gain in being
part of a community,
environmental gain
by building in timber,
and architectural gain
in access to generous
communal space.

The climate crisis asks for new relationships between:
· collective and individual spheres and responsibilities
· material and social care
· spatial organisation and relational behaviour patterns.
    Vindmøllebakken in Stavanger is a co-housing project which shows how these visible and invisible architectures can intertwine to support and build social ecological awareness and sustainable life practices. Siv Helene Stangeland, at the Norwegian practice Helen & Hard, discusses how this project was developed.

New roles for architects and architecture
Back in 2010, we created a vision named Gaining by Sharing (GBS), pointing at four areas of gain:
1. environmental
2. social
3. architectural
4. economical.
Based on studies of co-living projects in Scandinavia, Austria and Switzerland, a GBS co-living model was developed for the normal commercial housing market and for all ages and life situations.
    The model is based on slightly smaller than normal units, fully equipped and organised around generous and inspiring shared spaces, owned with an equal share by each unit. This was permitted as a result of a special regulation on a masterplan level, which gave flexibility in terms of unit sizes because of available communal space. The prerequisite for successful invisible architecture to function well is a facilitated user participatory process running parallel to the building process.
    In contrast to a normal housing project, people can join workshops early in the process to become familiar with the concept, influence their own apartment and suggest activities for the common areas. Most importantly, it is a chance to get to know each other and to engage in forming a future common home together.
    The GBS projects are built with prefabricated visible timber elements to create a good indoor climate, reduce CO_2 emissions and bring experiential qualities of nature into an urban context.

The pilot project
In the pilot project, 40 apartments were organised around 500 m² of shared facilities, with a communal gathering space and dining area at the centre. The private units, which follow a grid of approximately 7.5 x 7.5 m, are readable in the overall volumetric structure and adjust well to the small scale of traditional log houses around the site, allowing inhabitants to easily identify their own dwelling.
    The entrance is through a courtyard into a double-height, half-climatised hallway with plants and herbs growing ready for the

Illustration of the first Gaining by Sharing co-housing project in Stavanger.

Main entrance through the inner courtyard and the central communal space.

adjacent communal kitchen. There are also workshops, guest rooms and a lounge with a workstation and a sewing room. An amphitheatre marks the start of an open stairwell and galleries leading to the apartments and to the library and greenhouse on the rooftop.

The sequence of rooms are designed to create visual connections between spaces and people. Inhabitants can easily follow what is happening in the shared areas but can also choose to go from the street directly to their apartment, allowing freedom to engage in communal life as they wish. The sound insulation between apartments and communal space was prioritised, and solved with a double-wall system of prefabricated timber elements with airspace and gypsum.

Since opening, the community is rich and thriving, covering all ages and life situations.

Interest groups are self-organising to manage the use of shared spaces and facilities, including a workshop group, gardening group, social event group and many more. There is even a group which facilitates decision-making processes in the monthly meetings.

The groups are arenas for building social cohesion as well as for practising environmental impact by engaging in recycling furniture, general DIY and growing vegetables.

During the COVID-19 pandemic, a Health, Safety and Environment group was set up to find ways of maintaining social life within distancing rules and other safety measures. During the weeks of social restriction, the community has provided resilient solutions for living in a pandemic situation. Coordinated action in a well-organised community with spatial buffer zones between the private and public domain provided safe ground for behavioural patterns to cope with an extreme situation.

Supporting individual and collective responses to climate change

Architecture can transform and renew the threshold between individual and collective spheres and thereby affect responsibilities and responses in relation to climate action. The GBS co-living model does so both by its spatial structure and by its clear intention of sharing as a means to create a more sustainable everyday life, which in turn creates a meaningful common ground for the inhabitants. The spatial organisation is providing opportunities for collective action and practices of sharing. The timber material used in its construction is a constant reminder of the underlying intention of this project, as the inhabitants can support each other in making more sustainable choices and engage in creating the sustainable everyday life they want individually and together.

During the GBS user participation process organised in parallel with the project development there was an invitation to reflect about personal needs and preferences in relation to becoming part of a co-living community.

Questions were asked, such as:
· What is most important in my own apartment?
· What could I be willing to share or take responsibilities for outside my apartment?
· What do I wish to create together with my neighbours?

They have proven to be key to prepare for co-living.

Through this process we have seen that small adjustments in design solutions in the private unit can provide a big difference in well-being and influence the preparation for interaction in the community, such as lowering a window to fit the height of an inherited chair or integrating a loom. An elderly man said in an interview that 'it was just after having settled and become satisfied in my own apartment that I could start to engage myself in the shared spaces'.

Spatial organisation and relational behaviour patterns

The spatial organisation of GBS co-living projects provide a clear focus around what is shared. Outside the private unit is a shared zone owned together with other people. It is important to engage in making these areas work in a way that is meaningful for each inhabitant and at the same time to find agreements for the community as a whole. A dynamic and continuous negotiation between individual and collective needs is taking place – for instance, where to smoke. In the monthly meeting when everyone could see each other's concerns written on a board, no-one felt that formal rules were necessary, other than

Dinner in the central communal space, before and during the COVID-19 pandemic.

Plan layout of the ground
floor showing the central
communal space in the
very middle surrounded by
the half-climatised hallway
and all the private units
gathered around.

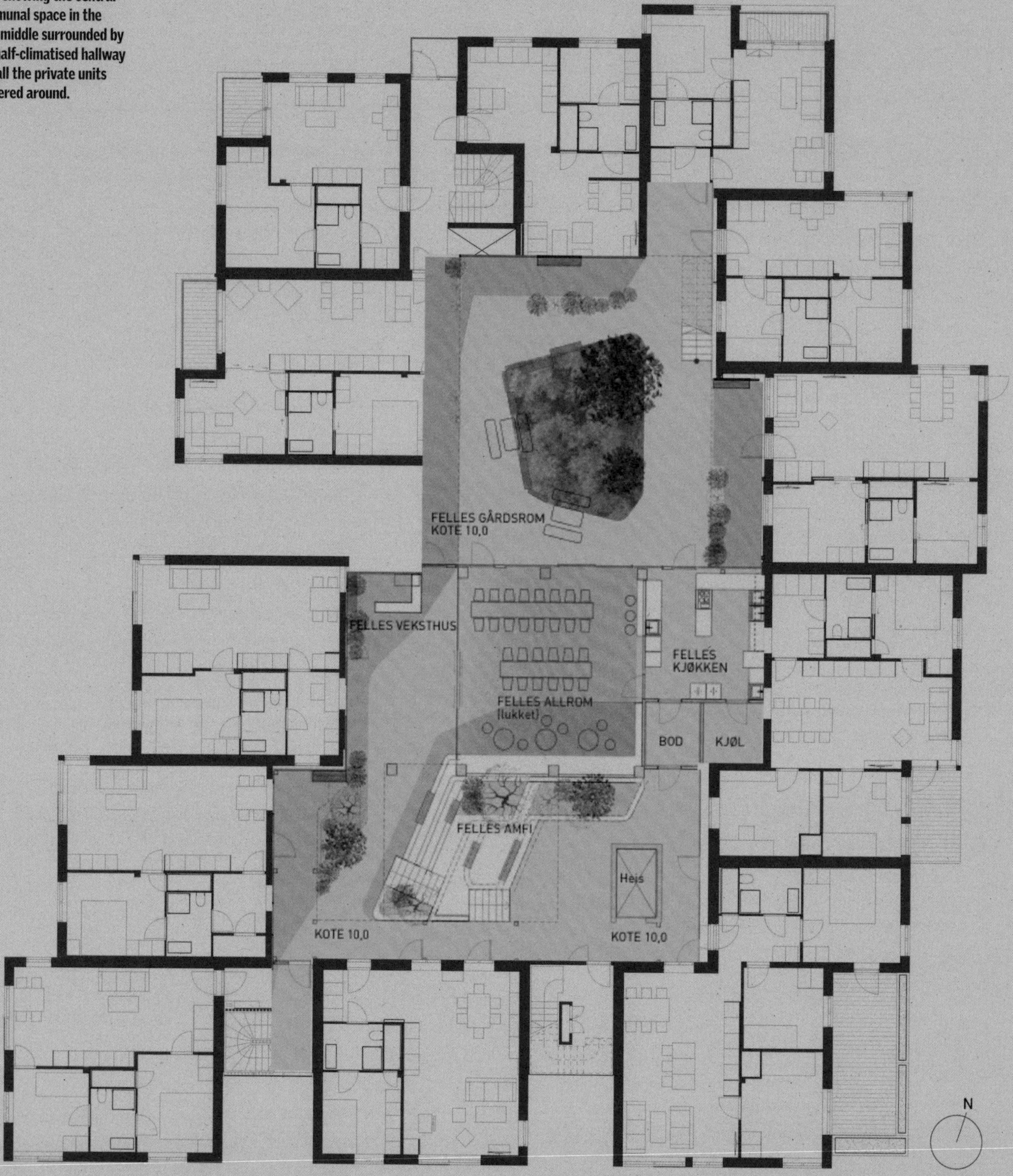

FELLES GÅRDSROM
KOTE 10,0

FELLES VEKSTHUS

FELLES ALLROM
(lukket)

FELLES
KJØKKEN

BOD

KJØL

FELLES AMFI

KOTE 10,0

Heis

KOTE 10,0

N

Compact Gaining by Sharing dwelling unit which has a customised furnishing solution whereby the bottom step continues to become a corner bench.

showing a high degree of consideration/respect for other co-livers. Flexibility and freedom of spatial occupancy and usage were prioritised over zoning and strict behaviour rules. Consensus agreements like this show the intrinsic relationships between spatial organisation, ownership, self-awareness and social sustainable behaviour.

Another example is that shared space attracts different activities and groups are forming around these activities. To make this overlapping use and set of interests work, there is both a need for spatial-material care and social care, which depend on each other.

For instance, the attic is a flexible space for a library, yoga, meditation, group gatherings, reading and games. On one occasion, the library group was taking up too much space with the result that the meditation activity was suffering. This was addressed by dialogues with each group to understand the real spatial needs. Together, they found out that most important requirement for the library group was not to throw away any books; the solution was to spread the library out in the whole house, placing books for cooking close to the kitchen, books for handcraft beside the workshops and so on. This resulted in a gain for all parties concerned.

What has become clear after evaluating the pilot is that the synergies and added values of sharing depend on manifold conditions working together. The economic model based on each unit buying extra shared space provides the possibility to create generous and inspiring architecture which supports sharing and inspires a social life. It also creates ownership and engagement in the shared spaces. The user participation process created an essential collective intention and expectation which seems to be a driver for practising Gaining by Sharing. These co-dependencies point at the importance of working on systemic levels to succeed with new transformative models for living.

The global climate crisis calls into question how we as architects can take on new roles and new collaborations while still inventing at the core of architecture. Gaining by Sharing is an example of how architects can introduce new concepts for living where spatial organisation and design qualities are helping people to focus on climate action while feeling empowered and enriched.

A member of the gardening group watering flowers in the shared greenhouse on the rooftop.

PROFILE:
Implementing Sustainability
Anders Lendager at Lendager Group

Upcycle Studios, Ørestad, Denmark; Resource Rows, Ørestad, Denmark; Olympic Pavilion, Tokyo, Japan; UN17 Village, Copenhagen, Denmark

Left: Lendager Group, Resource Rows, Ørestad, Denmark, 2019. Modern concrete mortar makes it difficult to separate bricks. The walls of Resource Rows are built using upcycled bricks cut out in 1 m2 sections and used directly in the new building.

To succeed with sustainability, the architect needs to be included in all the decisions, from the harvesting of materials, material innovation and material production to the final implementation of the materials in the design. In this profile, Anders Lendager discusses obstacles for sustainability and how to create results in the built environment through detailed profiles of Resource Rows, the Danish pavilion for the Tokyo Olympics, Upcycle Studios and UN17 Village.

Resource Rows, Ørestad, Denmark

Resource Rows was a housing project in Copenhagen with 92 flats arranged around a shared courtyard and roofscape, which included 29 greenhouses made from recycled wood and windows.

In taking on the project, Lendager Group wanted to create homes with their own history. Anders Lendager explains: 'When people migrate to the cities, they take all their possessions with them; so why not the buildings? We found that we could build new dwellings out of waste such as bricks and residual wood and we wanted to make them at no additional cost. Built largely from recycled materials, the scheme is two rows of three-storey terraced houses bookended by two five-storey apartment blocks. The project demonstrates a radical recycling approach to materials that significantly cuts construction carbon footprint.'

For example, the walls are built using upcycled bricks (cut out in 1 m² sections and used directly in the new building), taken from a demolished Carlsberg brewery and a school. As the brewery bricks were cement-mortared and difficult to disassemble, we developed a method where large squares would be cut from old facades. Brick modules in different colours are then put together in new designs, which gives the building a patchwork-like facade. Each brick represents a CO_2 saving of 500 g and the wood a CO_2 saving of 77%. All internal floors were made of Dinesen waste wood that would otherwise have been burned and all external wood is wood waste from the Metro construction.

Olympic Pavilion, Tokyo, Japan

Lendager Group won the prestigious Danish pavilion competition for the 2020 Tokyo Olympics (postponed due to COVID-19) with an ambition to design the most sustainable Olympic Pavilion in modern history. Anders Lendager expands on the process: 'In the early design phase, we looked into what Japanese people associate with Denmark. Two things stood out: design and craftsmanship. Outside Tokyo, there is a museum dedicated to Danish design chairs and we wanted to tap into that narrative. After stacking a handful of classical wooden dining chairs in the meeting room, we were convinced – we wanted to design the pavilion out of chairs!'

Lendager Group, the Denmark Pavilion for the Tokyo Olympics, Japan, 2021. The Danish pavilion for the Tokyo Olympics is a construction of 2,500 chairs made of plastic waste and residual wood – some from Fukushima. When the games are over, the pavilion will be taken apart and each chair will be sold and reused and will live on for many years to come, giving the pavilion an afterlife with minimal waste.

But, how do you combine sustainability with the prevailing Olympic legacy of abandoned hotels, stadiums, ski jumps and other sports facilities which across continents are now the decaying monuments of nine weeks of Olympic games?

Such abuse of resources is the result of linear thinking where the facilities have not been included in general city strategies, and the architecture has not been designed for disassembly or with materials that can be easily upcycled and used for other purposes.

The goal for the pavilion was that everything would be reused. For example, the chairs are made of plastic waste and residual wood from the Fukushima region which has had issues selling its wood after the 2011 nuclear disaster. When the games are over, the pavilion will be taken apart and each individually numbered and signed chair will be reused and live on for many years to come, giving the pavilion an afterlife with minimal waste.

The chair was designed as a module measuring 60 x 60 x 70cm from wood and waste plastic, including ocean plastic. The outside shape functions as a building block, and when mechanically joined the chairs can be used for walls and arches. Once separated, each object works as a chair – or actually two. In one direction, you have a dining table chair and, if you flip the object 180 degrees, it is transformed to a lounge chair. A total of 2,500 signed and numbered chairs will be available for sale.

The pavilion is built around the iconic Hibiya Park fountain in central Tokyo, embracing the fountain and creating a public space around it. As visitors enter through the huge arched openings, the technical aspect of the design – the chairs – reveals itself.

Upcycle Studios, Ørestad, Denmark

Upcycle Studios was the world's first large-scale upcycle project and its elegant townhouses attracted considerable attention when they were completed in 2018. As much as 75% of the windows come from abandoned buildings in North Jutland, Denmark and 1,400 tons of upcycled concrete was cast from durable concrete waste left from the construction of the Copenhagen Metro. The concrete was cast on site and 45% of its aggregate was concrete waste, representing a CO_2 saving of 13%. However, one of the largest savings is in waste reduction. Usually you order about 10% more concrete than you need, but the waste was reduced to almost zero by casting on site. The wood for the floors, walls and facades were produced using waste wood from the luxury wood manufacturer Dinesen, which represented a CO_2 saving of 77%.

The glass for the windows was sourced from an energy renovation that otherwise would have been discarded if it had not been upcycled. Originally made in 1999, it still had a life expectancy

Lendager Group, Upcycle Studios, Ørestad, Denmark, 2018. The facade is made from upcycled thermo windows in double frames and waste wood which has been burned on the surface and treated with linseed oil.

of 25 years and, through reclamation, gained new frames and new life. By combining the reclaimed glass in layers, the windows are as efficient as a modern three-layer window, and the glass alone represents a CO_2 saving of 87% compared to if made from virgin glass.

UN17 Village, Copenhagen, Denmark

UN17 Village is a construction project for around 400 new homes and apartments in Copenhagen, and the first in the world that aims to translate the UN17 Sustainable Development Goals (SDGs) into tangible action. If the visions are brought to life, it will be the most sustainable building project in the world according to UN Environment.

The project is still in the planning phase and on the way to realisation, therefore aspects may deviate from the original vision. However, the overall aims – to demonstrate how to build sustainable buildings by including building waste without compromising on quality, aesthetics, quality of life, sustainability, biodiversity, health, social responsibility and price – will remain unchanged. The aim is to construct the houses using as many upcycled materials as possible – including wood, concrete, glass, bricks, roof tiles, steel and possibly even industrial plastic waste – making it a project that taps into the circular economy. Lendager UP has developed upcycled materials designed for implementation on an industrial scale. The products always aims to be harvested and processed locally, creating local jobs and enabling the global construction of tomorrow's cities from today's waste.

The aim is not only to create an iconic and sustainable building from recycled materials, but also to create the opportunity for a sustainable way of life with a focus on health and community. For true sustainability, it will look at the whole lifecycle of the building, including the use of materials, health and quality of life.

According to the original plan, the UN17 Village consists of five buildings located in a manner to create an atmosphere of a village community. Most of the residents will be able to enjoy the sunlight from sunrise to sunset, enjoying the area's exceptional flora and fauna on their doorstep. The following sections explain how the competition proposal implemented each SDG. Real-life implementation may end up different as a result of project constraints and regulation.

Materials (SDG 4, 7, 8, 9, 11, 12, 17)

Future cities and buildings should not just be sustainable, they must be regenerative. If we are to create a better future, we must do away with the past. Denmark produces over 4 million tons of construction waste annually. This is the equivalent of 35% of all waste in the country. UN17 Village will be built of locally 'harvested' and upcycled materials such as wood, concrete and glass that will reduce CO_2 emissions by

between 50% and 97% on material level. Four of the five units will be constructed in timber and act as a carbon bank, and hopefully the last block will be built with a new kind of concrete that will reduce its CO_2 from between 20% and 30%.

Health (SDG 3, 4, 5, 6, 7, 10, 11, 13)

Buildings beat us to death; there can be no sustainability without health. Cities and buildings must be built so that it is healthy to live in them. UN17 Village aims to improve the quality of life of the residents by reducing the pollution of indoor air by ensuring an indoor climate that meets all aspects of physical and mental health and well-being. Poor air quality can result in anything from poor concentration to cardiovascular diseases and cancer. UN17 Village will increase the ventilation rate combined with high-quality filters and a choice of materials which minimise chemical fumes.

Community (SDG 1, 3, 4, 5, 10, 11, 13, 14, 16)

The idea is to create a community where residents can meet and form relationships. UN17 Village will create, amongst other things, 2,000 m² of communal areas, of which a large part is available for visitors. The village also aims to offer a bathhouse with pool, shared facilities, exchange

Lendager Group, UN17 Village, Copenhagen, Denmark, ongoing. UN17 Village is partly built with upcycled materials. The aim is not only to create an iconic and sustainable building from recycled materials, but also to create the opportunity for a sustainable way of life with a focus on health and community.

facilities, lobby and a guest house/dining house apartment hotel. For example, five flexible housing forms will meet changing family structures and future jobs, catering for a variety of family types, preventing it from becoming mono-functional. Further, communal roof terraces with exclusive access to the building's residents will create greater coherence and co-ownership of the buildings.

Biodiversity (SDG 1, 2, 3, 5, 8, 10, 11, 12, 13, 14, 15, 17)

The vision includes a regenerative landscape based on low maintenance, drought- and wind-tolerant local breeds, offering optimal conditions for the local rare and protected wildlife. Biodiversity will be increased by 50% through gardens and natural habitats on the roofs, with the possibility of both wet and dry natural biotopes on the ground. Green roofs covered with local flora will help to create natural habitats for birds. In addition, a large area zoned for common herbal gardens will increase biodiversity. A large part of the roof is formed also by a common greenhouse supplying vegetables to the communal dining house. On ground level, allotment gardens will provide additional gardening opportunities for the residents. Earth use minimises the need for artificial insulation.

Water (SDG 4, 6, 7, 8, 9, 11, 12, 13, 14, 15, 16)

The plans forecast that the buildings will potentially collect 1.5 million litres of rainwater annually. The water can be recirculated for recreational use – for example, for gardens and flushing the toilet. In addition, a communal laundry room can allow for clothes to be washed with the collected rainwater. The water is partly filtered naturally by plants in the village's streams and lakes, contributing to a cleaner water reservoir which will also provide breeding ground for local freshwater animals and insects. UN17 Village will collect enough rainwater to water all plants and to fill the reservoir and the streams between the buildings.

Energy supply

Energy consumption will be derived 100% from renewable energy sources, most produced locally and the rest sourced from external clean energy sources such as wind turbines. Energy for building operations including heat pumps is planned to be sourced from solar PV cells on the roof tops – combined with upcycled materials, energy production is providing the overall framework for a potentially negative carbon footprint on LCA level. Combined with the heat pumps, the energy system minimises energy consumption for overall heating. Excess heat can also be used to heat the soil in selected gardens, in order to ensure a longer growing season.

CASE STUDY:
A Choreography of Bricks

Samira Rathod

School of Dancing Arches, Bhadran, India

Samira Rathod Design Atelier, School of Dancing Arches, Bhadran, Gujarat, India, 2019. Conceived from the scribble of a child, a school of dancing arches.

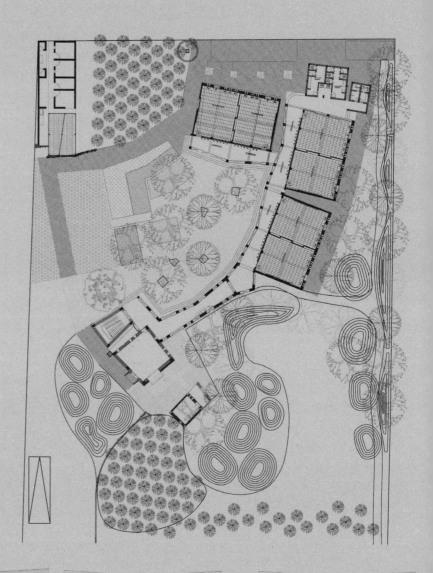

Architecture is an integration of form, space, experience, material and, most importantly, sustainability. Sustainability is about local materials, reuse, recycling, waste reduction and beauty. The School of Dancing Arches by Samira Rathod Design Atelier is an experiment in architecture and material, understanding local material, craft, construction techniques and passive energy techniques to reduce the carbon footprint in a localised manner – a direction towards the future. Made predominantly out of brick, the school is a collection of small spaces, all irregular in shape, that encourage imagination and play. The school is shaped in the form of a C, with a courtyard that provides self-shading and full of trees for further shade throughout the day. This case study explains the design of the building while making a case for craft, local material and technique as the way for architecture to be able to address the climate emergency.

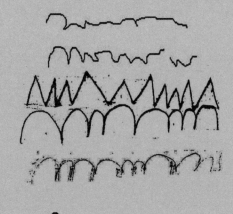

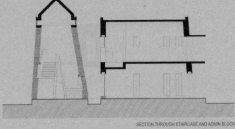

SECTION THROUGH STAIRCASE AND ADMIN BLOCK

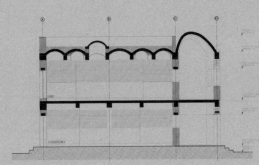

The architecture of freedom and questioning

Perhaps the closest memories we hold dear from our childhood are not of significant events but rather of insignificant events – losing oneself to wonderment, wandering under the skies and reliving vivid imaginations of the make-believe. This is the premise on which we began to design the spaces of the school at Bhadran, where a child spends its formative years, makes its first friends and etches its first memories.

The design was conceptualised from a child's scribbles that turned into a series of dancing arches. A scribble is indicative of not being instructed. It allows the freedom to express oneself in wavy, crooked lines in the only form a child knows. The dancing arches are a reminder of this freedom to satiate curiosities of the mind using imagination and wonder.

The design of the school: a child's scribble

Set on a plot of land surrounded by tobacco fields in the town of Bhadran, the design of the school grew organically. A series of classrooms dance their way through the trees, encountering alcoves, cracks and crevices, projections, niches and boxes, adding to a composition of experiences that would weave into the fabric of the school, much like the maze-like town of Bhadran itself.

Below: Samira Rathod Design Atelier, School of Dancing Arches, Bhadran, Gujarat, India, 2019.

The entire school is designed as a sequence of modules, and each module has a pair of classrooms and a corridor, with its tilted vaults strung sinuously. The height of the vaults and ridge roofs allow the hot air to rise and escape, and each classroom module is separated by an accessible gap, wide enough for cross-ventilation, which leaves the habitable spaces cool without the need for energy consumption through air conditioning. All the modules are designed to make repeated use of shuttering material made from waste steel and can be arranged in various patterns as deemed fit. Reuse of shuttering reduced the cost, while using fewer resources, and makes the building more sustainable. Roof forms are a sandwich structure with concrete in between layers of brick on the top and bottom. The classrooms have skewed beams with irregular jack arches, a unit of which protrudes to become a skylight. The roof is waterproofed with a thick layer of Brickbat Coba (broken brick pieces) in the profile of the arches, forming a playful broken brick landscape even on the roof. In the rain the terrace gets activated with water channels that trickle down into the landscape through spouts, percolating into the ground for conservation and reuse.

Samira Rathod Design Atelier, School of Dancing Arches, Bhadran, Gujarat, India, 2019. Dancing brick arches enclose the central courtyard.

Samira Rathod Design Atelier, School of Dancing Arches, Bhadran, Gujarat, India, 2019. Dancing arches in brick are made by using repetitive shuttering.

Landscape

The landscape, an undulating land mass
with a variety of tree groves, is an extension
of the same scribble. Children run through,
up and down the mounds and hide for their
peers to find them in such a landscape.
Plants are all local varieties, which grow
easily in the hot, dry climate of Gujarat. The
trees will have large shade-giving crowns in
a few years, creating spots of respite. The
mounds form a water channel, taking the
runoff to a soak pit for harvesting.

Samira Rathod Design
Atelier, School of Dancing
Arches, Bhadran, Gujarat,
India, 2019. The school
amidst the undulating
landscape.

**The brick floors in
the corridors can be
sprayed with water
on a regular basis to
keep them cool, an old
and local practice used
to keep verandas cool
in vernacular houses
during the summer.**

Samira Rathod Design Atelier, School of Dancing Arches, Bhadran, Gujarat, India, 2019. Brick has been used in walls, floors and roofs.

Materiality

Terracotta was predominantly used, with bricks – and only bricks – used in the walls, floors and roofs. Sourced from a kiln within 1 km of the site, the craft and labour of love lends the building its immaculate semantics and precision.

Brick: semantics and sustainability

Apart from an earthy appearance, the bricks as a building material come closest to resources already available in the environment, a material that will perish and go back to the environment, leaving no mark of destruction. This makes the local brick not just sustainable but also cost-effective for projects on urban peripheries in India. Brick is also a dense material, creating thick walls with high thermal mass. This property makes it an ideal material to avoid temperature fluctuations within the building in the hot and dry climate of Gujarat. While the outside temperature in the region could soar up to 45–48 degrees Celsius, the ambient temperature inside the school, as observed during and after construction, has been comfortable for human habitation. The brick floors in the corridors can be sprayed with water on a regular basis to keep them cool, an old and local practice used to keep verandas cool in vernacular houses during the summer.

While the brick properties prevent the heat from entering the spaces directly, the windows designed for the school are tall and narrow. Almost like slits, the wooden windows are frameless, saving cost, and on pivots so that they can be opened to allow cross-ventilation but minimise entry for dry, dusty, hot summer winds into the classrooms.

Light as a material

Light is a tangible building material which can be used as a needle to embroider moments and experiences in our architecture. The sharp dark shadows of the irregular arches in the corridor, the soft glow of tangerine through the lopsided vaults and the beams of light through the slits and skylights in the classroom add to this experience, generating intrigue. A building – a school – where the play of hide-and-seek is perpetual.

Samira Rathod Design Atelier, School of Dancing Arches, Bhadran, Gujarat, India, 2019. Staircase block with ridge roof and skylight.

CASE STUDY :
Adaptation Out of Necessity

*Anyana Zimmermann and
Fabián Rodríguez Izquierdo*

Cuba

While many countries still experience the problem of emotional and cultural denial of climate change, people in countries such as Cuba are already strongly affected by its impact. Yet those countries at the coalface of the climate crisis are a role model through their resilience. It starts with their approach: instead of focusing on the problem, Cubans search for the potential in the crisis. It is not adaptation due to a lack of resources, but to changing resources, to a changing climate and to changing disaster patterns. Ultimately, this adaptation invokes a changing mindset and a changing practice. The variety of pressing issues shows that designing and improving the built environment needs a holistic approach that adapts on different levels: environmentally, economically, socially. This article highlights the Cuban take on coping with the crisis as a reasonable balance between individual action-taking and innovative policy-making. It exemplifies what a global mitigation and adaptation agenda for a sustainable twenty-first century might look like.

Transformation of San Ignacio No. 360, Plaza Vieja, Old Havana, 2011. Extra walls and floors, so-called 'barbacoas', are inserted by the inhabitants to increase existing living areas.

Facades and stairs, Havana, 2011. Additional staircases built by the residents turn balconies into streets and extend the public space to the vertical.

Adaptation: Changing Resources

Resiliency is a Cuban tradition. Learning to cope with 60 years of material scarcity, generations of Cubans grew self-reliant and became prone to help each other to overcome obstacles. Their motto being 'Hay que inventar!' (You have to invent!).[1]

When there was neither space nor materials available, Cubans found a way of dealing with the shortage of living space. Urban growth occurred through transformation from within: by filling out, dividing, adding to and breaking through existing buildings, creating an urban density that allowed Havana to double its population in the past six decades.[2]

The break-up of the communist bloc in 1989, which had buffered Cuba against the restrictions imposed by the US, threw Cuba into a severe economic crisis. Heavily impacted by the sudden cut-off from imports, Havana turned into a role model of self-provisioning. Political measures, together with a decentralised movement of urban residents, created an urban food production strategy, boosting not only the economy but also improving public health and preserving biodiversity.[3]

Urban agriculture, Havana, 2019. The collapse of the Soviet Union led to massive import shortages for Cuba, including vital food, chemical fertilisers and fuel oil. Until today, a food production infrastructure is woven into Havana's city fabric by using almost every available square metre – from balconies to vacant properties – for organic farming.

Adaptation: Changing Climate

Today, the nation has been put to another test. Global warming increases already hot temperatures, resulting in a rising sea level and leaving the coastline more fragile than ever. The main danger of the changing climate is manifesting itself in coastal floods that are further exacerbated by extreme weather phenomena, which put the island's built and grown environment under even more stress.[4]

In 2017, the government approved a new adaptation strategy, the so-called 'Tarea Vida', which is implemented and controlled by the Cuban Ministry of Science, Technology and Environment.[5] This state plan collects tactical strategies and actions that look at prevention, preparation, response and recovery of vulnerable areas in the face of a changing climate, including progressive investments until the year 2100.[6]

The strategic measures prohibit the construction of new dwellings in threatened coastal settlements, reduce population density in low-lying areas and ensure that all new construction is well-adapted to the environment. Prioritising municipalities along the coastal line, the actions, to name but a few, include:

· the relocation of settlements
· the recovery of beaches, coral reefs, mangrove swamps and other natural protector ecosystems
· the improvement of infrastructures for an efficient use of water.[7]

It is also within the smaller-scale and urban realm that there is a shift in thinking. The new legal conditions of 2015, which fostered the realisation of individual projects, gave birth to 'Arbio jardines sostenibles'. This project was developed by two Cuban architects and focuses on the design, execution and maintenance of vertical gardens in Havana. Each garden creates a vertical ecosystem that consists of carefully selected – preferably autochthonous – native, species and elements that promote a positive reciprocal influence as a result of allelopathy.[8] The environmental benefits are numerous: functioning as a second skin, the vertical garden can reduce the surrounding temperature, increase air

Left: Vertical garden, Arbio jardines sostenibles (Raidel García Martínez and Alejandra Pino), Hostel Prado Restaurant, Havana, 2019. The structure for the vertical gardens consists of galvanised steel and cement panels, but the vision is to create panels from recycled materials (for example, plastic bottles or Tetra Paks) and to reach technological independence from imports through alliances with national companies. Although inexpensive during installation, one has to consider ongoing costs for maintenance and water consumption, which is why it has been mostly implemented in the private and commercial sector.[9]

Below: Deteriorating buildings, Havana, 2019. The empty corner plot is the result of a collapsed building during Hurricane Irma in 2017. It was chosen as one of the project sites for Anyana Zimmermann's masters thesis project and represents a series of empty building sites along Havana's seafront in Centro Havana.

quality and energy efficiency and contribute to the reduction of noise pollution and of urban heat island effect.[10] Its adaptability to alternative materials and the modular character allows this project to be expandable and even replicable in other countries.

Adaptation: Changing Disaster Patterns
Another very visible effect of global warming is the change in global storm patterns. Hurricanes have grown increasingly more devastating.[11] Despite its target location in the Caribbean Sea, Cuba has consistently experienced the lowest death tolls during hurricane season. This is due to deliberate foresight rather than a matter of luck. From the moment the Cuban Meteorological Service determines that a hurricane will hit land, the entire country has approximately 72 hours to prepare to 'welcome' it.[12]

There is also another reason for the country's successful education and evacuation system. For years, Cuba has studied the link between climate change and its adverse effects on mental health. As a result, in 2008 the Cuban Ministry of Public Health established the national Disasters and Mental Health programme. It incorporates resilience before, during and after severe weather occurrences. The programme identifies 'prevention' as the highest priority when confronting disaster situations, to ensure psychological and emotional recovery.[13]

For a natural event like a hurricane to actually become a disaster depends, among other reasons, on the physical and emotional capacity of the community to respond to it.[14] Centro Havana is the densest and one of the poorest neighbourhoods of the capital. It is characterised by an advanced deterioration of buildings and infrastructure, lack of open spaces and environmental pollution.[15] The effects of hurricanes, together with the lack of maintenance and overpopulation, have led to the progressive collapse of several buildings along the seafront, leaving adjacent facades exposed. Solid pavements foster the effects of flooding from the storm surge followed by heavy rains, and building erosion from salt-water.[16]

What if we pretend in the beginning of each project that our site – be it part of a neighbourhood, a village, a town, city, country – is in embargo? What materials do we have at hand? How can we reach self-sufficiency?

CURRENT STATE

The empty building plots leave adjacent building facades vulnerable. Wind turbulences occur especially in front of the northern building facades. The first building row along the Malecon (B) only slightly protects the buildings behind.

1ST COLLAPSE

After the first building collapse (B), the buildings behind are now fully exposed to the strong northern winds. Also the adjacent buildings' condition will degrade through the collapsed buildings due to the loss of structural support.

2ND COLLAPSES

A domino-effect is created: Slowly the wind will 'eat' its way through the urban fabric.

INTERVENTION: SOLID STRUCTURE

A building that fills in the current empty lots could create a wind breaker and reduce the wind impact on the adjacent buildings. A solid structure offers only a short protected zone and creates turbulences in front and behind the building.

INTERVENTION: PERMEABLE STRUCTURE

A permeable structure does not "break" the wind, rather it reduces the wind velocity and therefore reduces turbulences. By that it shields the adjacent buildings more effectively.

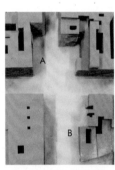
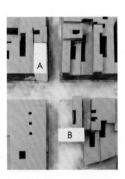
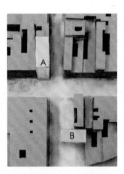

WINDSTILL

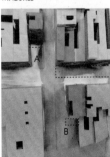
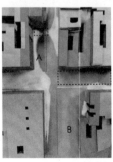
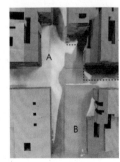
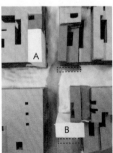

STRONG WINDS

N

NO WIND
WIND
VULNERABLE BUILDING
- - - TURBULENCES

A domino effect can be triggered if measures are not taken. Solid infills might protect adjacent facades, but they mainly redirect the wind and create turbulences. Permeable installations, on the contrary, reduce the wind speed and its impact on the surrounding buildings.[17] During the evacuation phase and depending on their building's condition, many people move either to neighbouring apartments or nearby shelters. As a hurricane hits, most furniture and household supplies on the ground floor are destroyed, and necessary infrastructure heavily damaged. Already overcrowded apartments become even fuller and already scarce resources even tighter. An improved built environment needs to absorb and reduce the incoming forces. It has to incorporate the layer of social infrastructure to protect not only physically but also to ensure emotional recovery and relief.

Adaptation: Changing Mindset

Our obsession for solidity and durability is challenged. The environment is shifting and so must our mindset. The Cuban palette of adaptations out of necessity could offer a very different point of view to disaster-resilient architecture: not only a reactive but also a proactive architecture that bends rather than breaks. This was explored in one of the author's masters thesis design project through

· a *permeable* architecture that shields and reduces the impact on both, buildings and people
· an *affordable* architecture that is made from local, cheap materials and can be grown and replicated
· a *repairable* architecture that is made from simple building methods and elements that could be easily replaced by the inhabitants themselves.

Actively inviting the community to take part in its construction and transformation helps to build pride and transfer knowledge, so that the building will be taken care of. Such an architecture of repair would reduce CO_2 emissions and support hurricane-resilient infrastructures both physically and socially.

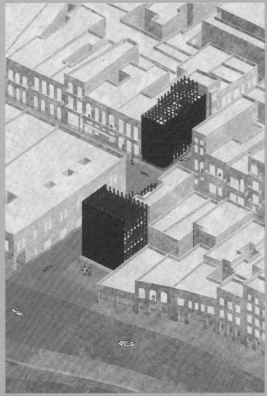

'Shield & Shelter', masters thesis project by Anyana Zimmermann, 2019. Before and after a hurricane passes, the bamboo structure and elevated concrete groundscape provide shadow and shelter with necessary facilities to promote various daily activities. During a hurricane, when everyone is evacuated, the facades close off and transform the bamboo structure into a windshield that reduces the incoming forces.

Adaptation: Changing Practice

The global climate emergency is calling for change. We must start by changing our approach. What if we pretend in the beginning of each project that our site – be it part of a neighbourhood, a village, a town, city, country – is in embargo? What materials do we have at hand? How can we reach self-sufficiency? Cubans show us that such a period of crisis represents an inspiration for rethinking political and economic structures to produce new spaces of sociability and encounter.

A new generation of architects must challenge conventional practice, which is developed with expensive materials and inadaptive techniques. Instead, we have to reveal the physical and aesthetic potential of the local context and help to expand the local knowledge of overseen – and often underrated – low-impact building materials. We need to see beyond the image of the 'informal' and translate its socio-economic procedures into operations that can inform a 'real' urbanism, truthful to the people's needs. We must mediate on a critical interface between top-down policies and bottom-up actions to allow us to free the concepts from their usual opposites and to let ourselves imagine new relationships. We have to consider architecture as a holistic approach that consists of both the built and the grown environment in order to generate new environmental, economic and social infrastructures.

It is in times of scarcity when new archetypes emerge. If we are in need of inspiration, it might be worth to ask ourselves: what would Cubans do?

Left and top right: 'Permeability vs Solidity', masters thesis project by Anyana Zimmermann, 2019. Neoclassical buildings with rows of columns create the facadescape of Havana's seafront. From afar, the bamboo structure seems solid, almost monolithic, like the surrounding colonial buildings, but a closer look reveals its permeability.

1 Aasa, M., Kongstein, M. & Oroza, E., *Editing Havana: Stories of Popular Housing*, Aristo Publishing, Copenhagen, 2011, p. 7.
2 Ibid, pp. 9-11.
3 Murphy, C., 'Cultivating Havana: Urban Agriculture and Food Security in the Years of Crisis ... Development Report No. 12.', *Food First*, Institute for Food and Development Policy, Oakland, CA, 1999, p. iv.
4 United Nations Development Programme – Climate Change Adaptation (UNDP), 'Cuba's Second National Communication', *UNDP*, https://www.adaptation-undp.org/projects/cubas-second-national-communication-progress, accessed 18 May 2020.
5 Expósito, M.L., 'Tarea Vida: un llamado a los hombres de ciencia en Cuba', *Ministerio de Educación Superior Cubano*, 2018, https://www.mes.gob.cu/es/noticias/tarea-vida-un-llamado-los-hombres-de-ciencia-en-cuba, accessed 8 May 2020.
6 Milán Y.R. & González Del Toro, D., 'Climate change brings transformations in Cuba', *GRANMA*, 2018, http://en.granma.cu/cuba/2018-04-12/climate-change-brings-transformations-in-cuba, accessed 18 May 2020.
7 Lorenzo, E.L.A., 'Tarea Vida', *EcuRed*, 2019, https://www.ecured.cu/Tarea_Vida, accessed 21 April 2020.
8 Martínez, R.G., 'Jardines Verticales' [email to F. Rodriguez Izquierdo], 19 May 2020.
9 Martínez, R.G., 'Jardines Verticales' [email to F. Rodriguez Izquierdo], 19 May 2020.
10 Basdogan, G. & Cig, A., 'Ecological-social-economical impacts of vertical gardens in the sustainable city model', *Yuzuncu Yil University*

Journal of Agricultural Sciences, Vol. 26, issue 3, 2016, p. 430.
11 Thompson, M., *Lessons in Risk Reduction from Cuba ... Case study prepared for Enhancing Urban Safety and Security: Global Report on Human Settlements*, Unitarian Universalist Service Committee, Massachusetts, 2007, p. 12.
12 Thompson, M., *Lessons in Risk Reduction from Cuba ... Case study prepared for Enhancing Urban Safety and Security: Global Report on Human Settlements*, Unitarian Universalist Service Committee, Massachusetts, 2007, p. 12.
13 Mesa, G. & Ortiz, P., 'Approaches to Climate Change & Health in Cuba', *MEDICC Review*, Vol. 17, issue 2, 2015, pp. 6-7.
14 United Nations, *2009 UNISDR Terminology on Disaster Risk Reduction*, United Nations International Strategy for Disaster Reduction (UNISDR), Geneva, Switzerland, 2009, p. 9.
15 Díaz, K.L. et al, *La adolescencia en La Habana Vieja. Su estado actual*, *Dirección de Gestión Cultural*, Dirección General de Patrimonio Cultural, Oficina del Historiador de la Ciudad de La Habana, Cuba, 2012, pp. 24-28.
16 Vã Zquez, D., 'Destruction Left by Hurricane Irma in Cuba Adds to Unease about the Effects of Climate Change', *University of New Mexico UNM Digital Repository*, 2017, https://digitalrepository.unm.edu/cgi/viewcontent.cgi?article=11470&context=noticen, accessed 28 May 2020.
17 Hyater-Adams, S. & DeYoung, R.J, Use of Windbreaks for Hurricane Protection of Critical Facilities, *National Aeronautics and Space Administration*, Langley Research Center, Hampton, Virginia, 2012, pp. 4-5.

CASE STUDY:
Sustainability is Not Enough

Stephen Choi

SBRC, University of Wollongong, Australia
Burnwood Brickworks, Melbourne, Australia
The Paddock, Castlemaine, Australia

The building design must consider the 'carrying capacity' of the site rather than usual practice, which is to 'build an object and then plug it in'.

NH Architecture, Burwood Brickworks, Melbourne, Australia, 2021. Project team members check in on the urban farm. The cafe greenhouse and sawtooth roof with solar PV stand in the background.

This article describes three different built projects involving the Living Future Institute Australia[1] that use the Living Building Challenge™(LBC™) framework to change the predominant narrative, radically re-framing our understanding of where we are, what we need to do and how we need to do it. Using the LBC™ – which is widely regarded as the world's most rigorous proven performance framework[2] – these projects demonstrate the possibilities for buildings of different sizes, geographies and typologies to be *regenerative*.

SBRC, University of Wollongong

The building

The Sustainable Buildings Research Centre (SBRC) is a multidisciplinary organisation that brings together researchers, students and industry at the University of Wollongong, 90 minutes south of Sydney. For its new 2,500 m² facility that needed to house offices, classrooms, laboratories and a high-bay warehouse, the client recognised the need to go well beyond the contemporary Australian environmental benchmarks.

Approaches and lessons

The brief in the LBC™ is simple: on an annual basis, generate more renewable energy than will be consumed. In other words, the building design must consider the 'carrying capacity' of the site rather than usual practice, which is to 'build an object and then plug it in'. Necessarily, there is a natural focus on passive design, but given all energy is considered, down to individual equipment 'plug-loads',[3] the consideration for the SBRC extended to other components, such as lighting control and 'green IT'.

A 160 kW rooftop solar photovoltaic array 'overproduces' during long summer days. Energy is therefore shared with the neighbouring student accommodation before excess power is exported to the grid. This arrangement involved infrastructure amendments at the site's main switchboard and allows the neighbouring building and the SBRC to share a single transformer, greatly improving the return on investment of the solar array. The team collaborated with the electrical utility, particularly in the development of approval processes, to enable PV arrays of this scale – bigger than residential but smaller than utility – to be accommodated.

The educational power of the project is most powerful. Energy usage is captured in detail and used for research. The design makes the roof proudly visible to the thousands of people passing each day.

Since the team knew the building would be 'net positive energy' in operation, the embodied carbon of the construction itself was first mitigated through a dematerialisation strategy whereby single products fulfilled multiple roles and other products were locally sourced and/or salvaged. The construction team was local, to reduce transport. The SBRC then fully offset the remaining embodied carbon.

Cox Architecture, SBRC, Wollongong, Australia, 2019. The rooftop solar photovoltaic array forms part of the sculptural aesthetic of the building form.

Cox Architecture, SBRC, Wollongong, Australia, 2019. The eastern aspect of the building shows the two wings connected by a landscape-hugged corridor. Salvaged timber reaches out from the building facade, inviting entry.

Burwood Brickworks Retail Centre

The building

Burwood Brickworks is a retail centre in a suburb 30 minutes east of Melbourne, home to a variety of uses including a supermarket, a cinema, a medical centre, a yoga studio, a childcare facility, fresh food outlets, restaurants and an urban rooftop farm, covering around 13,000 m². The project was initially subject to an international design competition,[4] which asked how a retail project of this nature could be 'ecologically restorative'.

Approaches and lessons

For a building with so many usages, the challenge was not only that tenancies are usually excluded in typical environmental ratings 'energy budget' but in determining how to accommodate and drive down the large variety of demands. To that end, the largest energy needs were refrigeration, space heating and cooling and lighting. Refrigeration cabinets have doors, which also provides an opportunity for reducing heating demands and makes heat recovery a possibility. In every single location within the building where a staff member would be located, an operable window, skylight or solar tube was integrated using a rather atypical approach to retail, providing fresh air,

daylight and views of the outside. A central mall space uses a sawtooth roof for optimum solar angles, while also incorporating glazing that opens and closes like a flower in response to external conditions.

'Food miles' are reduced through the installation of more than 5,000 m² of urban agriculture across the site, not only reducing food-related emissions but teaching visitors how to grow their own food whilst increasing the site's biodiversity. More than 100 crops are grown at any point in the year using a mixture of biodynamic and organic methods without the use of petrochemical fertilisers.

More than 50 salvaged materials show that it is better to upcycle products to both lower embodied carbon and to bring a sense of spirit to the place. In operation, wastewater is treated on site, more than a dozen separate waste streams are diverted from landfill and strong encouragement is provided to travel by tram, bus (via a newly-installed bus stop), bike or electric vehicle.

One of the important approaches for both managing energy and funding the project was to develop an embedded network, essentially creating a microgrid that allows for energy-sharing of the 1.1 megawatt solar array. The remaining electrical needs are met through off-site additional renewable energy, directly associated with the project.

NH Architecture, Burwood Brickworks, Melbourne, Australia, 2018. After the world's first Living Building Challenge™ design competition for a retail centre, the design incorporated a rooftop urban farm alongside a pedestrianised urban plaza.

NH Architecture, Burwood Brickworks, Melbourne, Australia, 2019. The retail centre roofscape undertakes to capture solar energy, to channel direct daylight and fresh air, and to create a connection to the sky.

NH Architecture, Burwood Brickworks, Melbourne, Australia, 2019. The central mall shows artwork that connects occupants to Country,[5] and glazing that responds to external conditions.

The Paddock Eco-Village

The project

The Paddock is a project that comprises 27 homes, plus a community centre, in Central Victoria. Open market terraced homes are set amongst land dedicated to a shared orchard, planted wetlands and native gardens. The vision is to create a new standard for scalable housing that fosters a sense of community and closer connection to nature. Like the other projects shown here, the Paddock aims to connect people to the natural world in a very direct way. The result is that if one is continuously close to something, one is far more likely to care for it.

Crosby Architects, The Paddock, Castlemaine, Australia, 2019. Operable windows on the appropriate facades provide daylight across the seasons.

If one is continuously close to something, one is far more likely to care for it.

Crosby Architects, The Paddock, Castlemaine, Australia, 2019. An immediate connection with the natural environment encourages occupants to understand their part within it, and in turn care for it.

Crosby Architects, The Paddock, Castlemaine, Australia, 2019. The first phase of market homes terracing down towards a shared wetland that supports the natural hydrological cycle.

1 *Living Future*, https://living-future.org.au/, accessed 15 June 2020.
2 *Living Future*, 'Program Evolution', https://living-future.org/lbc/basics4-0/#what-does-good-look-like, accessed 15 June 2020.
3 Simply speaking, the energy used by products that are powered by means of an ordinary AC plug.
4 *Living Future*, 'Brickworks Living Building Challenge', https://living-future.org.au/the-brickworks-living-building-challenge-design-competition/, accessed 15 June 2020.
5 For many indigenous people, land relates to all aspects of existence – culture, spirituality, language, law, family and identity. Each person is entrusted with the knowledge and responsibility to care for their land, providing a deep sense of identity, purpose and belonging. This deep relationship between people and the land is often described as 'connection to Country'.

Approaches and lessons

One of the market attractions to these homes is that they are highly energy efficient, with the intent that each property produces more clean energy than it uses once occupied. Over 4 kW of solar panels power each of the all-electric properties before excess energy is fed back into the grid. Hot water and space heating are powered by electric heat pumps. Ceiling fans are installed throughout and a single split system is used for exceptional heating and cooling.

Beyond the physical systems, the project recognises that the key to net-positive energy is in understanding how people live. Shared gardens, connecting footpaths, leisure areas, solar-powered electric bike charging and a laundry with external clothes lines were developed as a result of workshopping with future residents. A spare bedroom in a shared community centre is booked by residents for their guests, in lieu of every single household having an extra bedroom used for only a few nights in any given year. When not used by the guests, income from renting rooms in the community centre reduces shared running costs.

When neighbours know each other, it makes sense that they feel more secure, making it more likely that residents actually open the windows, curtains and/or blinds for free heating, cooling, airflow and daylight. Design flexibility of the homes allow intensification of use and ageing-in-place, reducing occupant turnover. The second storey of each home can operate independently with toilets, kitchenette and private access.

Final Word

According to Kate Raworth's Doughnut economics model as referenced by three of our contributors, our job as a society is to meet the basic human rights of everyone on the planet without overshooting the boundaries of what our world is capable of supporting. It may seem like an obvious target, yet we have learned that our current economic model does not even have this goal at its core.

If our collective worth is rated according to our growth, regardless of the damage it causes us or the basic needs we require, is it surprising that we are failing so miserably to stay within the safe boundaries?

Architecture is a human right ...

As humans we have basic needs and fundamental rights, as set out in the United Nations Universal Declaration of Human Rights. It includes the right to adequate standards of living, housing and places to educate ourselves and our children. We have the right to participate in the cultural life of a community, the right to rest and relaxation and the right to protect ourselves at tribunals.

To achieve these basic needs and standards for the billions of people on the planet as Al Borde and raumlabor have found, we cannot help but make make architecture, but Architects must take this duty seriously and humbly to act in the service of others.

... but architecture is not above human rights

One of our most fundamental rights as humans is the right to life, liberty and security of person. Our planet has vital life-support systems which uphold the rights of the untold lives on this planet, and so our architecture must not be permitted to transgress these rights. As a species, we declare that human beings are all born free and equal in dignity and rights, but this also means that it is not permissible for architecture's impact in one demographic to affect the lives of those in another. Yet, this is what has been happening for decades. We must call it out and hold that society to account with conviction.

Architects can no longer deny global citizenship and must take a global passport into the office to permeate projects with solidarity and consciousness.

Power together

We cannot change system level problems by working in our own design silos, both in terms of our discipline but also in terms of the physical confines of our projects, outside which we must operate together to find better solutions. A metaphor of this can be found in Sambuichi's work with the traditional construction on Naoshima where, instead of working as a disjointed series of obstacles and blocking out the wind, structures operate as a single breathing organism, to the benefit of all.

We must work on a micro and macro level if our work is to form part of the solution. We must create spaces for conversation – on a community, regional and ecosystem level – and design intelligent, low-impact and locally sensible systems.

Design like you are in an embargo

We have also seen designers and practitioners coming to terms with the dichotomy of creating more from less. No clearer than Zimmermann and Rodríguez Izquierdo's study of Cuba, where a small island nation isolated from the world around it had had no choice but to stay within its immediate ecological boundaries. The resulting practices form a microcosm of the change that we need as a society, questioning the idea that architecture must be a new building, or even a building at all.

Sustainability is not enough

If we do decide to build as we have seen from Choi, sustainability is not enough: doing less harm is not the same as doing no harm. We need current and future architects to commit to going beyond this: we can no longer be sustainable in some areas while neglecting others. We need consistently high standards in all aspects. We need to develop a new kind of holistic and regenerative architecture that leaves the world in a better position than when we found it, and where the individual parts and aspects are closely interconnected and important enough to be taken as a whole.

Our final 'crit' is approaching

In this volume, we have been faced with information that has been difficult to accept and which challenges our ability to practise architecture. Yet, we have seen that we have all the tools we need to redesign our framework to suit the new normal.

As well as our practice, our education needs to change, and it can. The initiatives and organisations shown have started as embryonic entities of change. They are notably different from, and yet intrinsically connected to, the conventional institutions they challenge, creating a new momentum that we must seize.

Everything needs to change

If this volume has illustrated why everything must change, it has also shown that there is a will for everything to change. The many practitioners, activists, students and educators are each taking on their own part of the problem and working together to find common solutions.

Contributors have shown that designing for change and for a more sustainable tomorrow does not mean that our architecture is at the expense of beauty and delight or architectural creativity. Indeed, quite the opposite.

Yet, we challenge all of you, including all of us as contributors, to study and reflect on the content of this volume and acknowledge that each of us still have gaps in our own work. The designs and ideas presented are inspirational and far-reaching, yet all of us need to reach further.

The time for discussion is long over. It is now the time for collective and – even more than ever before – creative action.

As Greta Thunberg reminds us:
'Our house is on fire.'
'Everything needs to change.'
'And it has to start today.'

Extinction Rebellion's Protest Towers using Bamboo
and Tensegrity principles to blockade Rupert Murdoch's
Printing Presses. Dezeen's Phineas Harper suggested
these structures 'recall the sustainable motives of high-
tech architecture and should win the Stirling Prize'.

Contributors

Nacho Ruiz Allen is an assistant professor at the Aarhus School of Architecture, Denmark, and has taught at several universities in Spain. He studied architecture at Universidad de Navarra, Pamplona and at Universidad Politécnica de Cataluña, Barcelona. Since 2012, he has held a PhD on architectural theory from Universidad Politécnica de Madrid.

Architects Climate Action Network (ACAN) is a diverse and fast-growing campaign group of individuals within architecture and related built environment professions taking action to address the twin crises of climate and ecological breakdown.

Dr Andrew Barrie is an Auckland-based designer and Professor of Design at the School of Architecture and Planning at the University of Auckland. He is a regular contributor to architecture and design journals and has exhibited extensively nationally and internationally. His design work has won numerous awards in both New Zealand and Japan.

Tom Bennett is an architect at Studio Bark, university tutor and climate activist with Extinction Rebellion (XR). In April 2019, he was one of over 1,000 people arrested for participating in non-violent civil disobedience. In 2019, he helped to launch the Architects Climate Action Network (ACAN).

Stephen Choi is a project architect whose work has included the development of environmental assessment methods, designing and managing buildings, embedding sustainable development into educational curriculum, and being a global Living Building Challenge™ expert. Several of his projects – both private and public – have gained wide recognition for progressing green building.

Elizabeth Donovan is an assistant professor at the Aarhus School of Architecture, Denmark, where she gained a PhD within the field of sustainable architecture. She also studied architecture at Victoria University of Technology in New Zealand and Chalmers Institute of Technology in Sweden.

Thomas R. Hilberth is a Swiss-educated architect and Associate Professor at Aarhus School of Architecture, Denmark. He is the coordinator for research and teaching in Emerging Sustainable Architecture. He holds a PhD in his research field of architecture and security, and is founding partner of Hilberth & Jørgensen Arkitekter.

Satu Huuhka is an architect and a Doctor of Science in Architecture. She works as a senior research fellow in Tampere University, School of Architecture, where she has also taught refurbishment, renovation and conservation. She has dedicated her career to advancing the circularity of construction, contributing to evidence-based theory, policy and practice.

Fabián Rodríguez Izquierdo is an architect graduated from the School of Architecture of the Technological University of Havana, Cuba. He has worked in a small office applying the concept of adaptive re-use, learning how old existing architecture can endure and transform according to current time specifications. This will help us to define future designs in order to coexist with the environment and influence it in a more positive way.

Mario Kolkwitz was born in Mannheim, Germany and acquired his bachelor's degree in architecture in 2016. After gathering hands-on experience in working as a roofer, carpenter and architect, he moved to Finland to finish his studies at Tampere University to pursue his goal of creating architecture with purely positive impact.

Urszula Kozminska has been working as an architect in Warsaw and Amsterdam since 2005. She holds a PhD in circular economy in architecture. She has been teaching at several universities in Poland. Currently, she is an assistant professor at the Aarhus School of Architecture.

Kari Kytölä is a recent architecture graduate from Tampere University. Having written his thesis about reclaimed materials in architecture, he is interested in interdisciplinary connections between architecture and fashion as well as weaving sustainability and reclamation into practice. He currently works at Team for Resilient Architecture (TREA) in Helsinki.

Anders Lendager is CEO and founder of Lendager Group, which successfully implements sustainability in the build environment. The practice has established itself as one of the strongest and most influential companies in Denmark in the upcycling and circular economy.

Elina Luotonen is currently working on her masters degree in sustainable architecture at Tampere University, Finland, and attained her bachelor's degree in architecture in 2015. Her interest in urban practices, civil activism and human environmental impact was gained through living in major global cities and rural areas on three continents.

Dorte Mandrup is founder and Creative Director of her eponymous practice. Studies in both sculpture/ceramics and medicine have influenced her approach to architecture, which has always been 'hands-on'. Her design philosophy and artistic, yet systematic, mindset permeate the entire office as she is design responsible for all projects. Dorte headlined at the curated international exhibition at La Biennale di Venezia in 2018, is Vice Chairman of the Louisiana Museum of Modern Art, Chair of the prestigious Mies van der Rohe Award 2019, and holds frequent visiting professorships abroad.

Mikhail Riches is an architecture studio led by David Mikhail and Annalie Riches. Clients include local authorities around the UK as well as developers such as Urban Splash and Town. The studio has committed to delivering low-carbon projects going forward. In 2019, the practice won the Stirling Prize for their Passivhaus Goldsmith Street development in Norwich.

Kasia Nawratek is a senior lecturer at Manchester School of Architecture. She is an architect, academic and writer. Her current research interests are focused on Anthropocene and Speculative Design Practices in the context of architectural education. In her teaching, she uses narrative as a design generating tool and, following Mikhail Bakhtin's idea of polyphony, fosters an inclusive and dialogic studio culture.

Alex de Rijke is a founding director of dRMM Architects. He is responsible for the concept, design and delivery of key timber projects. These include diverse works such as Sliding House, Kingsdale School, Charlton WorkStack, Tower of Love, Endless Stair, WoodBlock House, Maggie's Oldham, and the Stirling Prize winning Hastings Pier.

Paulina Sawczuk is a recently qualified architect from Poland, currently based in Finland, where she graduated from Tampere University. She gained professional experience in Hanover and Helsinki, where she has worked for Lahdelma & Mahlamäki Architects, and she constantly searches for inspiration in Nordic architecture and design.

Siv Helene Stangeland is a Norwegian architect and researcher who founded the architectural office Helen & Hard in 1996 with Reinhard Kropf. The practice is known for its research on sustainable timber architecture and has an extensive body of built work. In 2017 Stangeland and Kropf were awarded the RIBA's International Fellowship.

Kongjian Yu (DDes at Harvard Graduate School of Design) is a professor and the Founding Dean of Peking University College of Architecture and Landscape, and founder of the practice Turenscape. His projects have won numerous international awards including 12 ASLA Awards. He is a member of the American Academy of Arts and Sciences and Fellow of the American Society of Landscape Architects.

Anyana Zimmermann graduated as an architect from the Aarhus School of Architecture in Denmark, where she further worked as a research and teaching assistant at the department of 'Emerging Sustainable Architecture'. Recently shifting from the academic to the professional world, she now explores and questions her own role as an architect in contemporary society. She wonders: how can the built environment repair the threads that connect us to the grown environment, to communities, to empathy?

Recommended Reading

Books

Extinction Rebellion, *This is Not a Drill: An Extinction Rebellion Handbook*, Penguin, 2019.

Fitz, Angelika, *Critical Care: Architecture and Urbanism for a Broken Planet*, The MIT Press, 2019.

Hamin Infield, Elisabeth M., Abunnasr, Yaser and Ryan, Robert L., *Planning for Climate Change: A Reader in Green Infrastructure and Sustainable Design for Resilient Cities*, Routledge, 2018.

Hawken, Paul, *Drawdown: The Most Cozmprehensive Plan Ever Proposed to Roll Back Global Warming*, Penguin, 2018.

Hawkes, Dean, *The Environmental Imagination: Technics and Poetics of the Architectural Environment*, Taylor & Francis, 2019.

Hopkins, Rob, *From What Is to What If: Unleashing the Power of Imagination to Create the Future We Want*, Chelsea Green Publishing, 2019.

Kellman, Ilan, *Disaster by Choice: How Our Actions turn Natural Hazards into Catastrophes*, Oxford University Press, 2020.

King, Bruce, *The New Carbon Architecture: Building to Cool the Climate*, New Society Publishers, 2017.

Klein, Naomi, *This Changes Everything: Capitalism vs. The Climate*, Simon & Schuster, 2014.

Maathai, Wangari, *The Green Belt Movement: Sharing the Approach and the Experience*, Lantern Books, rev. 2004.

Lewis, Simon and Maslin, Mark, *The Human Planet: How We Created the Anthropocene*, Penguin Books, 2018.

Pallasmaa, Juhani and Zambelli, Matteo, *Inseminations: Seeds for Architectural Thought*, Wiley, 2020.

Pawlyn, Michael, *Biomimicry in Architecture*, RIBA Publishing, 2011.

Raworth, Kate, *Doughnut Economics: Seven Ways to Think Like a 21st-Century Economist*, Penguin Random House, 2017.

Saad, Layla F., *Me and White Supremacy: How to Recognise Your Privilege, Combat Racism and Change the World*, Quercus, 2020.

Singha, Sumita, *Autotelic Architect: Changing World, Changing Practice*, Routledge, 2016.

Thackara, John, *How to Thrive in the Next Economy: Designing Tomorrow's World*, Thames and Hudson Ltd, reprint 2017.

Thunberg, Greta, *No One Is Too Small to Make a Difference*, Penguin, 2019.

Till, Jeremy, *Architecture Depends*, The MIT Press, 2009.

Wallace-Wells, David, *The Uninhabitable Earth: A Story of the Future*, Penguin, 2019.

Watson, Julia, *Lo-TEK, Design by Radical Indigenism*, Taschen, 2019.

Journals, articles and reports

Bendell, Jem, *Deep Adaptation*, jembendell.com/2019/05/115/deep-adaptation-versions/

Climate Emergency Design Guide, and Net Zero Operational Carbon Paper www.leti.london/

IPCC report and summaries, www.ipcc.ch/sr15/

Klinsky, Sonja and Mavrogianni, Anna, 'Climate justice and the Built Environment', Climate Justice: The Role of the Built Environment, Buildings and Cities, 2020, journal-buildingscities.org/articles/10.5334/bc.65/

UN Sustainable Development Goals, 'Transforming Our World: The 2030 Agenda for Sustainable Development', sustainabledevelopment.un.org/post2015/transformingourworld

Organisations and initiatives

Anthropocene Architecture School, www.patreon.com/AnthropoceneArchitectureSchool

Better Block: Disruptive and Creative Placemaking, www.betterblock.org

Living Building Challenge, living-future.org/lbc/

ARCH4CHANGE, Digital climate change curriculum for architectural education, www.arch4change.com

Index

Page numbers in **bold** indicate figures.

AAction 73
Aalto, Alvar 29
activism see architectural activism
Al Borde 57–65, **58**
    Casa Culunco, Tumbaco, Ecuador **64–65**
    Comedor de Guadurnal, Guadurnal, Ecuador 58, **59**
    'Dark Resources', Venice Biennale, Italy 63, **63**
    Esperanza Dos, Manabí, Ecuador 58, **60**
Amateur Architecture Studio
    Ningbo History Museum, Ningbo, China **29**, 30
Andersen, Christian 84, **84, 85**
Andreassen, Malthe 82, **82**
Anthropocene 90, 96
Anthropocene Architecture School 67, **67, 68**
Apuzzo, Francesco **58**
Aravena, Alejandro 63
Architect NRT
    Harald Herlin Learning Centre, Espoo, Finland **28**, 29
Architects Climate Action Network (ACAN)
    activism 42, **42–43**, 73
    aims 67
    Education group 66–67, **66**, 73, 75
Architects Declare 40, **40**
Architects Registration Board (ARB), UK 73
architectural activism 34–45, 73
    Anna Heringer 38
    Architects Climate Action Network 42, **42–43**
    Architects Declare 40, **40**
    Covent Garden Community Association 36–37
    eight steps towards 44
    Extinction Rebellion 41, **41, 42–43**
    Eyal Weizman 39
    Santiago Cirugeda 38
    Torange Khonsari 39
architectural education 64–65, 66–75, **71, 74**
    activism and lobbying 73, 75
    carbon-neutral design 70
    collaboration 70–72
    environmental design 69
    state of play 67–68, **67, 68, 69, 72**
    sustainable architecture 76–85, 77–85
    see also Ecosystem City Studio, Sheffield School of Architecture
Architecture Foundation 105
Australia
    Burnwood Brickworks, Melbourne 140, **140, 141**
    The Paddock Eco-Village, Castlemaine 142–143, **142, 143**
    Sustainable Buildings ResearchCentre (SBRC), University of Wollongong 139, **139**

Bader, Markus 58–65, **58**
Bakhtin, Mikhail 88, 94
Barragán, David 58–65, **58**
Bath Climate Action Group 73
Belgium
    EUROPA-Building, Brussels **24–25**, 31
Benavides, Esteban **58**
Benyus, Janine 40
biodiversity 123
Birmingham School of Architecture and Design EARTH group 73
Blackmore, Daniel 41
Borja, Marialuisa 58
Braungart, Michael 26
Building Schools for the Future programme, UK 105
Burnwood Brickworks, Melbourne, Australia 140, **140, 141**
Buro Happold 100
Büscher, Bram 87

Canada
    Fountain House, Montreal **61**
Capitalocene 93, 96
care, feminist methodology of **90–91**, 93–94
carnivalesque 94–95
Casa Culunco, Tumbaco, Ecuador **64–65**
Causse, Toya 84, **84**
Centre for Alternative Technology, Wales 73
Centre for Contemporary Nature 39
Chamberlayne, Isabelle 94–95, **96, 97**
China
    Dong'an Wetland Park, Jiyang District, Sanya City, Hainan Island **53**, 54–55
    Meishe River corridor, Haikou City, Hainan Island 49–54, **50, 51**
    Ningbo History Museum, Ningbo **29**, 30
    Sanya Mangrove Park, Sanya, Hainan Island **46–47, 52**, 54
Chthulucene 96
circular economy 26, **26**
    see also upcycling and reuse
Cirugeda, Santiago 38
City of York Council housing, UK 101–103, **102, 103**
civil disobedience 41
Clay Field, Suffolk, UK **98**, 99–100, **99, 100**
co-living/co-housing 82, **83, 110–115**, 111–115
Comedor de Guadurnal, Guadurnal, Ecuador 58, **59**
community engagement **56–65**, 57–65
Construction Declares 40
Convivial Conservation 87
Covent Garden Community Association (CGCA) 36–37
COVID-19 pandemic 87, 96
Cox Architecture
    Sustainable Buildings ResearchCentre (SBRC), University of Wollongong, Australia 139, **139**

critical thinking 25–33, **26**
    RETHINK 27, 29–31
    THINK AHEAD 27, 31–32
    THINK TWICE 27–29
Crosby Architects
    The Paddock Eco-Village, Castlemaine, Australia 142–143, **142, 143**
cross-laminated timber (CLT) 70, **104**, 108–109, **108, 109**
Crutzen, Paul 90
Cuba
    adaptation to climate change 130–137, **130–137**
    disaster resilience 133–135, **133, 134, 135**
    student design projects 78, 79–80, 79, 81–82, **81–83**
    urban agriculture 131, **131**
    vertical gardens 132–133, **132**

Dalton, Ruth 67, 68, 69, 70, 73
Danish Olympic Pavilion, Tokyo, Japan 117–120, **118–119**
'Dark Resources', Venice Biennale, Italy 63, **63**
Darmstadt, Germany 62
Denmark 3–4
    Lisbjerg Bakke housing, Aarhus 31, **31, 32**
    Løgstør **76–77**, 79
    Lønstrup 80, **80**
    Resource Rows, Ørestad **116**, 117
    student design projects **76–77**, 79, 80, **80**, 83–84, **83–85**
    Sundbyøster Hall II, Copenhagen, **10**, 11, **11**
    UN17 Village, Copenhagen 121–123, **122–123**
    Upcycle Studios, Ørestad 120–121, **120–121**
    Vejle 83–84, **83–85**
    Wadden Sea Centre, Ribe, **4–7**, 5–7
Derbyshire, Ben 67, 68, 73
Devlieger, Lionel 29
disassembly and relocation 31–32, **31, 32, 33**
Dong'an Wetland Park, Jiyang District, Sanya City, Hainan Island, China **53**, 54–55
Dorte Mandrup Arkitekter
    Ilulissat Icefjord Centre, Ilulissat, Greenland **1, 2–3**, 5
    Sundbyøster Hall II, Copenhagen, Denmark **10**, 11, **11**
    Trilateral Wadden Sea World Heritage Partnership Centre, Wilhelmshaven, Germany **8, 9**, 11
    Wadden Sea Centre, Ribe, Denmark **4–7**, 5–7
Doughnut economics model 87
dRMM
    Kingsdale School, London, UK **104–109**, 105–109

ecological infrastructure see Sponge City
Ecosystem City Studio, Sheffield School
   of Architecture **86**, 87–96, **88–97**
Ecuador
   Casa Culunco, Tumbaco **64–65**
   Comedor de Guadurnal, Guadurnal 58, **59**
   Esperanza Dos, Manabí 58, **60**
education see architectural education
embodied carbon 99, 101, 102–103
energy
   consumption 3–4, 123
   passive solar design **98**, 99–100, **99, 100**
   renewable 123, 139, **139**, 140, **140**, 143
environmental footprint 4–5
Esperanza Dos, Manabí, Ecuador 58, **60**
EUROPA-Building, Brussels, Belgium
   24–25, 31
Extinction Rebellion (XR) 41, **41, 42–43**, 73

feminist methodology of care **90–91**, 93–94
feminist theory 90
Finland
   Harald Herlin Learning Centre, Espoo
   28, 29
   Vanhankaupungin Kellokas housing,
   Helsinki **30**, 31
Fisher, Berenice 93
Fletcher, Robert 87
Floating University Berlin, Germany
   56–57, 64
Flores & Prats Architects
   Sala Beckett arts centre, Barcelona, Spain
   27, 28
Foerster-Baldenius, Benjamin 58
Forensic Architecture 39
Fountain House, Montreal, Canada **61**
France
   Grand Parc Bordeaux 8
Friedman, Milton 87
Fukutake, Soichiro 13, 17, 19

Gaining by Sharing (GBS) co-living projects,
   Norway **110–115**, 111–115
Gangotena, Pascual **58**
Germany
   Darmstadt **62**
   Floating University Berlin **56–57**, 64
   Haus der Statistik, Berlin **61**
   Trilateral Wadden Sea World Heritage
   Partnership Centre, Wilhelmshaven, **8, 9**, 11
Gerstenberg, Frauke **58**
Giddings, Joe 42
global warming 2–3
Goldsmith Street, Norwich, UK 100–101,
   100–101
Graham, Stephen 93
Grand Parc Bordeaux, France 8
green infrastructure see Sponge City
Greenland
   Ilulissat Icefjord Centre, Ilulissat, **1, 2–3**, 5

Hainan Island, China **46–47**, 49–55, 50–53
Harald Herlin Learning Centre, Espoo, Finland
   28, 29
Haraway, Donna 96
Haus der Statistik, Berlin, Germany **61**
Heatherwick Studio
   Zeitz Museum of Contemporary Art Africa,
   Cape Town, South Africa 28, **28**
Helen & Hard
   Vindmøllebakken Co-housing Project,
   Stavanger, Norway **110–115**, 111–115
Heringer, Anna 38
Heydron, Niclas 82, **83**
Hiroshima, Japan 19–23, **23**
Hofmann, Andrea 58
Hong Kong **34–35**, 41
Howland, Alice **94–95**, 95

Ilulissat Icefjord Centre, Ilulissat, Greenland
   1, 2–3, 5
Intergovernmental Panel on Climate Change
   (IPCC) 2
Inujima Seirensho Museum, Inujima Island,
   Japan 17–19, **20–21, 22**
Italy
   'Dark Resources', Venice Biennale 63, **63**
Itsukushima Shrine, Miyajima Island, Japan
   13, **14–15**, 17, 23

Japan
   Danish Olympic Pavilion, Tokyo 117–120,
   118–119
   Hiroshima 19–23, **23**
   Inujima Seirensho Museum, Inujima Island
   17–19, **20–21, 22**
   Itsukushima Shrine, Miyajima Island
   13, **14–15**, 17, 23
   Miyajima Misen Observatory, Miyajima
   Island **12**, 13–17
   Naoshima Plan, Naoshima Island 19, **23**
   Orizuru Tower, Hiroshima 23, **23**
   Rokko Shidare Observatory, Kobe **16**, 17, **18**
Jitendhar, Sanjukta **86**, **88–93**, 93–94
JKMM Architects **28**

Kangeisai Festival, Japan 13
Karin Krokfors Architects
   Vanhankaupungin Kellokas housing,
   Helsinki, Finland **30**, 31
Khonsari, Torange 39
Kingsdale School, London, UK **104–109**,
   105–109
Klause, Johann 82, **82**
Klein, Naomi 41, 70, 87
Krischanitz, Adolf 31–32, **33**

Lacaton & Vassal
   Grand Parc Bordeaux, France 8
Lendager Group
   Danish Olympic Pavilion, Tokyo, Japan

117–120, **118–119**
   Resource Rows, Ørestad, Denmark **116**, 117
   UN17 Village, Copenhagen, Denmark 121,
   122–123
   Upcycle Studios, Ørestad, Denmark
   120–121, **120–121**
Liesegang, Jan **58**
Life Cycle Assessment (LCA) 4, 5
Lisbjerg Bakke housing, Aarhus, Denmark
   31, **31, 32**
Living Building Challenge (LBC) framework
   Burnwood Brickworks, Melbourne,
   Australia 140, **140, 141**
   The Paddock Eco-Village, Castlemaine,
   Australia 142–143, **142, 143**
   Sustainable Buildings ResearchCentre
   (SBRC), University of Wollongong,
   Australia 139, **139**
Løgstør, Denmark **76–77**, 79
Lønstrup, Denmark 80, **80**
Lyhne, Mads 82

McAulay, Scott 67–68, **67, 68**, 70
McDonough, William 26
Martin, Sir Leslie 106
Masdéu, Josep 27
material resources
   cross-laminated timber (CLT) 70, **104**,
   108–109, **108, 109**
   disassembly and relocation
   31–32, **31, 32, 33**
   flexibility and adaptability **30**, 31–32
   materials in context 4–7
   renovation and retrofitting 8, 26, **26**,
   27–29, **27, 28**, 105–107, **106, 107**
   upcycling and reuse 7–8, 29–31, **29**, 116,
   117–122, **118–123**, 140
Mayer, Christof 58
Meadow, Donella 40
Meishe River corridor, Haikou City,
   Hainan Island, China 49–54, **50, 51**
Mies van der Rohe Award 8
Mikhail Riches
   City of York Council housing, UK 101–103,
   102, 103
   Clay Field, Suffolk, UK **98**, 99–100, **99, 100**
   Goldsmith Street, Norwich, UK 100–101,
   100–101
Miyajima Misen Observatory, Miyajima
   Island, Japan **12**, 13–17
Modern Art Museum of Warsaw, Poland
   31–32, **33**
Monahan, Jim 36–37
Moore, Jason W. 93

Naoshima Plan, Naoshima Island, Japan
   19, **23**
neoliberalism 37
Nguyen, Phuong Uyen 82
NH Architecture

Burnwood Brickworks, Melbourne, Australia 140, **140, 141**
Ningbo History Museum, Ningbo, China **29**, 30
Nordvik, Frida 84, **84**
Norway
    Vindmøllebakken Co-housing Project, Stavanger **110–115**, 111–115

Orizuru Tower, Hiroshima, Japan 23, **23**

The Paddock Eco-Village, Castlemaine, Australia 142–143, **142, 143**
participatory design **56–65**, 57–65
passive solar design 98, 99–100, **99, 100**
Passivhaus 100–103, **100–101, 102, 103**
Pawlyn, Michael 40
Penn, Joe 42
Poland
    Modern Art Museum of Warsaw 31–32, **33**
polyphony 88, 96
Public Works 39

radical participatory design **56–65**, 57–65
rainwater collection 123
raumlabor 57–65, **58**
    Darmstadt, Germany **62**
    Floating University Berlin, Germany **56–57**, 64
    Fountain House, Montreal, Canada **61**
    Haus der Statistik, Berlin, Germany **61**
Raworth, Kate 40, 87
Recetas Urbanas 38, **38**
recycling see upcycling and reuse
regenerative design 40, 123, 138–143, **139–143**
renewable energy
    123, 139, **139**, 140, **140**, 143
renovation and retrofitting 8, 26, **26**, 27–29, **27, 28**, 105–107, **106, 107**
Resource Rows, Ørestad, Denmark **116**, 117
reuse see upcycling and reuse
Rokko Shidare Observatory, Kobe, Japan **16**, 17, **18**

Sala Beckett arts centre, Barcelona, Spain **27**, 28
Sambuichi, Hiroshi 12–23
    Inujima Seirensho Museum, Inujima Island 17–19, **20–21, 22**
    Miyajima Misen Observatory, Miyajima Island **12**, 13–17
    Naoshima Plan, Naoshima Island 19, **23**
    Orizuru Tower, Hiroshima 23, **23**
    Rokko Shidare Observatory, Kobe **16**, 17, **18**
Samira Rathod Design Atelier
    School of Dancing Arches, Bhadran, India 124–129, **124–129**
Sampson, John 73

Samyn & Partners
    EUROPA-Building, Brussels, Belgium **24–25**, 31
Sanya Mangrove Park, Sanya, Hainan Island, China **46–47, 52**, 54
School of Dancing Arches, Bhadran, India 124–129, **124–129**
Shackleton, Hugo 80, **80**
Sheffield School of Architecture (SSoA)
    Ecosystem City Studio **86**, 87–96, **88–97**
    Students for Climate Action 67, 70, 73
Shevills, Lauren 42
Skelcher, Cith 73
Sønderland, Isak D. 83–84, **83**
South Africa
    Zeitz Museum of Contemporary Art Africa, Cape Town 28, **28**
Spain
    Sala Beckett arts centre, Barcelona **27**, 28
Sponge City 47–55
    concept 48–49
    ecosystem services 48, 55
    Hainan Island projects, China **46–47**, 49–55, **50–53**
Stirnemann, Florian **58**
Stokkeby, Marleen **76–77**, 79
Studio Bark 41, **41**
Sundbyøster Hall II, Copenhagen, Denmark **10**, 11, **11**
Sustainable Buildings Research Centre (SBRC),University of Wollongong, Australia 139, **139**
sustainable design 2–11
    community engagement and working locally **56–65**, 57–65
    cross-laminated timber (CLT) 70, **104**, 108–109, **108, 109**
    disassembly and relocation 31–32, **31, 32, 33**
    embodied carbon 99, 101, 102–103
    experimentation 8–11
    flexibility and adaptability **30**, 31–32
    implementation of SDGs 121–123
    materials in context 4–7
    passive solar design **98**, 99–100, **99, 100**
    Passivhaus 100–103, **100–101, 102, 103**
    political action 3–4
    rainwater collection 123
    regenerative design 40, 123, 138–143, **139–143**
    renewable energy 123, 139, **139**, 140, **140**, 143
    renovation and retrofitting 8, 26, **26**, 27–29, **27, 28**, 105–107, **106, 107**
    towards zero carbon architecture **98–103**, 99–103
    upcycling and reuse 7–8, 29–31, **29, 116**, 117–122, **118–123**, 140
    urban agriculture 131, **131**, 140, **141**

using evidence 4–7
vertical gardens 132–133, **132**
Sustainable Development Goals (SDGs) 121–123

Taller General **59**
Thallaug, Ida 82
Thrift, Nigel 93
Thunberg, Greta 36, 145
Timm, Axel 58
Trilateral Wadden Sea World Heritage Partnership Centre, Wilhelmshaven, Germany **8, 9**, 11
Tronto, Joan C. 93
Turenscape see Sponge City

UN17 Village, Copenhagen, Denmark 121–123, **122–123**
United Kingdom
    City of York Council housing 101–103, **102, 103**
    Clay Field, Suffolk **98**, 99–100, **99, 100**
    Goldsmith Street, Norwich 100–101, **100–101**
    Kingsdale School, London **104–109**, 105–109
University of Science and Art (UCAL), Lima, Peru 64
University of the Arts, Berlin, Germany 64
Upcycle Studios, Ørestad, Denmark 120–121, **120–121**
upcycling and reuse 7–8, 29–31, **29, 116**, 117–122, **118–123**, 140
urban agriculture 131, **131**, 140, **141**

Van Roey, Wanda **78**, 79–80, **79**
Vandkunsten Architects
    Lisbjerg Bakke housing, Aarhus, Denmark 31, 31, 32
    Vanhankaupungin Kellokas housing, Helsinki, Finland **30, 31**
Vejle, Denmark 83–84, **83–85**
Venice Biennale 2016, Italy 63, **63**
Venturini, Gianpiero **71**
vertical gardens 132–133, **132**
Vindmøllebakken Co-housing Project, Stavanger, Norway **110–115**, 111–115

Wadden Sea Centre, Ribe, Denmark **4–7**, 5–7
Wahl, Daniel 40
Wang Shu **29**, 30
Weizman, Eyal 39
Westervik, David 81–82, **81**

Zeitz Museum of Contemporary Art Africa, Cape Town, South Africa 28, **28**

Image credits

ii–iii
Unsplash / Callum Shaw
vi–vii
Guy Reece 2020 @Strikingfaces
x–3
Image by Mir
4–7
Adam Mørk
8
Image by Mir
9
Dorte Mandrup
10–11
Adam Mørk
12
Sambuichi Architects – special permission was obtained to take the photograph of Miyajima Misen Observatory published in this book
14–23 top
Sambuichi Architects
23 bottom
Shinkenchiku-sha
24–25
Flickr / Fred Romero (corno.fulgur75)
26
Kari Kytölä & Paulina Sawczuk
27
Ricardo Flores / photo by Adrià Goula
28 top
Wikimedia Commons / Axxter99
28 bottom
Tuomas Uusheimo
29
Wikimedia Commons / Siyuwj
30
Karin Krokfors
31
Anne-Mette Manelius / photo by Helene Høyer Mikkelsen
32
Anne-Mette Manelius
33
Radosław Nowik / Museum of Modern Art in Warsaw
34–35
ZUMA Press, Inc. / Alamy Stock Photo
36–37
Jim Monahan
38 top left
Santiago Cirugeda / Juan Gabriel Pelegrina
38 top right
Studio Anna Heringer
38 bottom
Santiago Cirugeda / Recetas Urbanas
39
Forensic Architecture in collaboration with FIBGAR, 2017
40
Michael Pawlyn

41
Natasa Leoni
42–43
Matthew Rosier
46–53
Kongjian YU / Turenscape
56–57
Pierre Adenis
58 left
Al Borde
58 right
raumlabor berlin
59
JAG Studio
60
Esteban Cadena
61 top
Nils Koenning
61 bottom
raumlabor
62
Studio Rustemeyer
63
Al Borde
64–65
JAG Studio
66
ACAN
67–68 top
Scott Macaulay
68 bottom–69
ACAN
71
Gianpiero Venturini
72–74
ACAN
76–77
Marleen Stokkeby
78–79
Wanda Van Roey
80
Alexander Hugo Shackleton
81
David Westervik
82 top
Johann Klause
82 bottom
Malthe Andreassen
83 left
Niclas Heydron
83 right
Isak Sønderland
84 top
Toya Causse
84 bottom–85
Christian Andersen
86–93
Sanjukta Jitendhar
94–95
Alice Howland

96–97
Isabelle Chamberlayne
98–99
Tim Crocker
100 top
Mikhail Riches
100 bottom–101
Tim Crocker
102–103
Mikhail Riches
104
dRMM / photo by Alex de Rijke
105
dRMM / sketch by Alex de Rijke
106 top
dRMM / photo by Alex de Rijke
106 bottom–107
dRMM / sketch by Alex de Rijke
108
dRMM / photo by Michael Mack
109
dRMM / photo by Farid Karim
110
Sindre Ellingsen
111–112 left
Helen & Hard
112 right
Sindre Ellingsen
113
Minna Suojoki / Helen & Hard
114
Helen & Hard
115 top
Sindre Ellingsen
115 bottom
Helen & Hard
116–123
Lendager
124–125 top
Niveditaa Gupta
125 bottom–129
Samira Rathod Design Atelier
130
Ernesto Oroza
131
Anyana Zimmermann
132
Raidel García Martínez
133–137
Anyana Zimmermann
138
Stephen Choi
139
SBRC
140 bottom
Tom Graham, Xplore Photography
140–141
Frasers Property
141 bottom
Dianna Snape

142 top
S.J. Royle
142 bottom–143
Neil Barrett
146–7
Extinction Rebellion / Gareth Morris